ELEMENTS OF LIVING™

BIG HOME, BIG CHALLENGE

DESIGN SOLUTIONS FOR LARGER SPACES

Kira Wilson Gould

with Saxon Henry

McGraw Hill Professional

The McGraw·Hill Companies

Cataloging-in-Publication Data is on file with the Library of Congress

1 2 3 4 5 6 7 8 9 0 PUR/PUR 0 9 8 7 6 5 4 3

ISBN 0-07-142248-X

The sponsoring editor for this book was Cary Sullivan and the production supervisor was Pamela Pelton.

Printed in China by Print Vision.

McGraw-Hill books are available at special quantity discounts to use as premiums and sales promotions,
or for use in corporate training programs. For more information, please write to the Director of Special
Sales, McGraw-Hill, 2 Penn Plaza, New York, NY 10121-2298. Or contact your local bookstore.

The book is printed on acid-free stock.

ELEMENTS
OF LIVING™

Packaged by Elements Media, a division of Third Republic Media, LLC.
President/Creative Director: Chris Kincade
Editorial Director: Kira Wilson Gould
Art Director: William van Roden

Elements of Living is a trademark of Third Republic Media, LLC.

Third Republic Media, LLC
16 West 19th Street, Tenth Floor
New York, NY 10011

TITLE PAGE Designed by Dick Clark Architects.
OPPOSITE Designed by Noel Jeffrey.
TABLE OF CONTENTS Designed by Bobby McAlpine.

DEDICATION

For my husband, Gordon, and daughter, Kylan, who present me with the biggest challenges, but also the greatest rewards.

— K.W.G.

ACKNOWLEDGEMENTS

First and foremost, I would like to thank all of the experts—the designers, architects, contractors, artisans, et al—for sharing their time, knowledge and projects with us. This book would not have been possible without them. Of course, I am equally indebted to Cary Sullivan, my editor at McGraw-Hill, and Chris Kincade of Elements Media for championing this project. Even though her name is on the cover, my co-author, Saxon, deserves a special mention here because she jumped to the task with enthusiasm and no questions asked. Special thanks to my mother—she's a tireless editor and full of great ideas. Also, as a new mother myself, I could not have completed this book without the dedication of my daughter's nanny, Rebecca Artley. And finally, much love and thanks to my husband for his patience and understanding as I tackled this great challenge.

TABLE OF CONTENTS

Challenge: Make a large house not look like one large mass;
Solution: Design one section to look like an addition.
Designed by Moore Ruble Yudell Architects.

THE BIG HOME CHALLENGE

Houses in America are getting bigger. Reporting on the latest Census Bureau statistics, *The New York Times* claims that the "celebrated prosperity of the 1990s brought a surge in the size and values of homes." This new breed of house—the

one with the large, double-height foyer, the standard three-car garage and the giant family room/kitchen combination—is becoming more common. In California, Texas and Florida, houses seem to have no limits in terms of size; it's not uncommon to find houses in the 10,000-, 20,000- or 30,000-square-foot range. And we're not just talking about the suburbs. In urban settings, the popularity of loft-style apartments is unrivaled. Old manufacturing buildings, as well as traditional residential buildings, are being converted into spaces with super-high ceilings and open-floor plans.

With the size of our homes increasing, there's a growing concern that we're creating houses that are over-the-top, out-of-scale and generally uninhabitable. After all, a person is only so big! Things naturally fit better and feel more comfortable when they're created in proportion to the human figure. When you start tampering with the scale of architecture and furnishings, you can very easily move beyond the comfort zone. Think of the architecture of a grand cathedral with its vaulted ceilings: when you walk in, you feel small and insignificant. This, of course, is what the great architects of history had in mind when they envisioned these exalted spaces—you were supposed to feel awed. However, this is presumably not the feeling you want to create in your family room.

Some of these new houses are so vast, and the materials so impersonal (think miles of polished marble),

Challenge: Break up a large living space while still maintaining a sense of connection; Solution: Build partitions, but keep a line of visual axis. Designed by DD Allen.

ADDRESSING THE ISSUE

the end result is reminiscent of a hotel lobby. Perhaps it's nice to look at, but would you want to live there? Does it feel like home? One interior decorator we spoke with likened the phenomenon to "having your morning coffee in a bowling alley." Another says these new homes are so big and out-of-scale that they look like they've been "pumped full of air."

How do we tackle this big space challenge? Researching our own design dilemmas, we couldn't help but notice the lack of resources devoted to the subject. There is an abundance of books about designing or decorating a small space: how to make the most of your small space, how to live large in a small space, and so on. But what about those of us who live in large spaces? (And we don't necessarily mean the entire

ABOVE Challenge: Make triple-height ceilings seem less imposing; Solution: Treat the top portion of walls the same as the ceiling to visually lower it. Designed by Sidnam Petrone Gartner. OPPOSITE Challenge: Properly light expansive living room; Solution: Use a wide variety of lighting, including task and ambient. Designed by David Easton.

"A lot of people are attracted to the super-large rooms when they're buying a house. But if comfortable and reassuring places haven't been created, it's human nature to want to close in a bit after the initial thrill of being in the super-large room." — MATTHEW PATRICK SMYTH

house: Your large space may be a double-height foyer that feels too tall or a long hallway that seems to go on forever.) How do we live large, yet comfortably? How do we navigate the fine line between magnificent and out-of-scale?

These questions inspired us to write *Big Home, Big Challenge*. Our goal is to shed some light on the problems of building and/or living in large spaces, and to provide detailed solutions—both architectural and decorative— that take your needs and surroundings into consideration. Through examples, you'll discover how a well-designed great room can feel more intimate and inviting than a smaller, but poorly conceived one. In the following pages, we'll help you turn your large space into one that's as comfortable and inviting as it is breathtaking.

INTRODUCING THE EXPERTS

There are as many ways to solve the challenges that accompany the process of building, renovating or updating a large home as there are people who design and build them. To better understand the variety of approaches, we spoke with dozens of leading interior designers, architects,

contractors and other design professionals, spending countless hours with some of the best minds in the business. We visited their studios, walked through their projects in progress, scoured through their portfolios and toured some of their homes. Our objective was to harness their knowledge into concise insights that would help readers tame their own unwieldy spaces.

In *Big Home, Big Challenge*, we elaborate on the experience of these experts, translating it into in-depth solutions for creating successful furniture groupings, effective lighting, harmonized paint and wallpaper treatments, essential architectural elements, personalized artwork and accessories and more. And since the property surrounding a large home is as important to consider as its interiors, we include tips from top landscape designers on how to coordinate outdoor spaces with indoor rooms. Throughout the book, you'll also find "Inside Feng Shui" tips written by Feng Shui master and interior designer Benjamin Huntington. These primers explain how the ancient Chinese art of placement can help make a room feel friendly and inviting.

As we explore the most critical elements necessary to lend a home personality and create a successful design scheme, we put our findings at your fingertips— each chapter ends with a "punch list" similar to those used by architects and general contractors to evaluate whether a project is progressing as it should. These punch lists are convenient summaries that highlight the important points covered in each chapter. And finally, to help you in your quest to create a warm and inviting home, we've also included an appendix of our favorite resources.

As you turn the page and read about how to get started, we want to wish you luck and great success on the challenges ahead that will ultimately transform your big home into your ideal home.

PREVIOUS PAGE Challenge: Keep miles of countertop from becoming monotonous; Solution: Vary materials, introducing wood for a table-like feel. Designed by Sidnam Petrone Gartner. ABOVE Challenge: Accommodate varying numbers of people comfortably in a large room; Solution: Create several seating areas. Designed by Jose Solis Betancourt.

OPPOSITE Challenge: Make a tall stairhall comfortable without compromising its transitional function. Solution: Add visual interest with recessed paneling—tempered by not paneling every wall or making it full height, and playfully alternate between inset shapes. Designed by Glenn Gissler.

Treating the entry foyer as a garden room is a wonderful
opportunity to incorporate elements of the outdoors inside,
creating a harmonious transition. Designed by Mark Hampton.

GETTING STARTED

The design process starts with you. As the owner, you are the only one who can decide what kind of home you want, and how much you are willing or able to pay for it. Making sure that your lifestyle and the habits of family members are

considered during the planning process will ensure that your home suits your needs, and knowing how you want to live will help you understand how your home should be planned or changed. A trained architect, interior designer or design contractor can take your ideas and, working within the parameters of available resources, turn them into reality. But you must be actively involved in developing a well-thought-out game plan.

The first step is to map out the changes you wish to achieve. What improvements would you like to make? Are you building from scratch or remodeling? Can you simply redecorate, or does the entire floor plan need an overhaul? How is the exterior of the house—do you like the look of it? Does it relate to the locale and the style of the surrounding houses? Do your interiors relate to what's outside? What decorative style will you use? Favorite colors? These are just some preliminary questions. There are a host of tough questions that you must answer rigorously in order to determine the scope of the project, and to uncover your own sense of style.

While the answers to the important design questions will be different for everyone, one goal seems to be universal: regardless of style, we all want our personal space to feel intimate. When working on a large project, the number one priority is quite often introducing a sense of coziness. "People today do not live like they did a century or two ago," says high-end contractor Howard Chezar.

"They don't want to live in a huge, formal mansion, with whole sections of the house (such as the kitchen) treated as separate domains to be run by a staff of servants." Today, Chezar, who works in New York City and the Berkshires of Massachusetts, finds that his clients want homes that are large and commodious, but still livable, personal and individualized.

Soft fabrics and textured throws lend a sense of informality to a rich, paneled living room. Designed by Ilemeau et cie.

SPATIALLY CHALLENGED

To create that comfortable, yet modern home, you will need to determine your best course of action, and decide whether it includes smart decorating touches or intensive renovations. But, before you choose your design method, it is important to understand the basics of how space can be divided successfully to create a cozy interior.

As New York City architect Coty Sidnam explains, "There are ways—whether they're subliminal or very real—to delineate between the spaces in a large room." Sidnam is referring to both architectural and decorative solutions for subdividing a room, or creating specific areas of interest within a space. You do not necessarily have to view a large, open room as a single space (e.g., a dining room lined with bookcases is also a library);

A structural-looking partition separates the kitchen from the dining area in this Manhattan loft. Designed by Jeffrey Cole.

depending on how many functions the room will serve, it could be two or three distinct spaces (e.g., the same room can be used as an informal eating area, a play room and even a study).

Creating more defined areas, in fact, can often solve the big space challenge. Variations in wall coloring or floor patterns, or architectural elements such as railings can create the feeling of separate and distinct spaces—without actually building any walls. Even if you can't lower the ceiling in the living room, you can paint the top of the wall the same color as the ceiling, creating the illusion of lower ceilings and thus greater enclosure. In the following chapters, we look in-depth at all of the various ways to define space.

"You can define space by erecting four walls, but you can also imply space by using various elements of design." — JAY HAVERSON

VISUAL REFERENCE

Once you've outlined your basic design needs and determined whether you will build, renovate or decorate, you can then turn to the important task of assembling a visual reference library. The old adage "a picture is worth a thousand words" is quite apt when it refers to home design. Countless design experts extoll the benefits of pictures. Architect Jeffrey Cole says, "I often have clients cut things out of magazines. This is invaluable, as it helps me to know what a client likes or dislikes—a picture lets me see what they cannot articulate."

Like Cole, many designers advise their clients to collect reference files or create idea scrapbooks. East Hampton interior designer Zina Glazebrook gives her clients this all-important homework. "I'm pretty adamant that you determine what people's habits are and how they like to live by getting them to tear pages from magazines or mark pages in coffee-table books," Glazebrook explains. "This exercise gives me a feel for the styles that they love. As I see the different things they're collecting, something will emerge that will allow me to really 'get' where they are coming from."

Though style considerations are best addressed after functional issues, an idea folder can be started at any time during a project. Even if you are months or years away from building or renovating, collecting visual inspiration and filing the pages away in a special folder will serve you well when you are ready to delve into your project. Whether you fan the images on your desk as you plan the project yourself, or pore over the pages with the professionals you choose, you'll be ahead of the game when it comes to ensuring that your home speaks to your needs and your sensibilities.

ALTERNATIVE WAYS TO DEFINE SPACE

- Change of color
- Change of elevation
- Change of finish on walls
- Use of architectural details, such as beams, coffers, wainscoting and columns
- Variation in floor texture, finish or pattern
- Modulated lighting
- Changes in ceiling planes
- Grouping of furniture
- Use of rugs to define areas

Repeating certain motifs and shapes, such as these oval-topped mirrors and this curved console table, help the eye move through the space, adding visual interest. Designed by Benjamin Noriega-Ortiz.

CULLMAN & KRAVIS' TIPS ON ORGANIZING A PROJECT FROM START TO FINISH

"The main challenge is to not have the project be overwhelming," says New York interior designer Elissa Cullman. Large homes and large rooms run the risk of appearing daunting—not just to live in, but also to decorate. How do you tackle what seems to be a big-scale problem? Where do you start, and how do you manage the process? Cullman's firm has spent years perfecting the art of designing large homes, and offers some helpful tips on how to organize the project.

- Ask yourself and your family a series of questions about your project, including questions about function, style and budget.

- Find inspiration both through reading materials (magazines, books, brochures) and site visits (designer show houses, historic homes, botanical gardens).

- Keep detailed reference files (or binders) with photo clips from design magazines and other visual reference sources.

- Take an inventory of all existing furniture and include photographs and measurements.

- Create a furniture floor plan for each room (you can buy furniture templates or software); if you don't have a floor plan, take photographs of each wall of a room and jot down the measurements on the back.

- When shopping for furniture and fabrics take floor plans or room photographs, a measuring tape and a paint color wheel (you can purchase one from Benjamin Moore). The color wheel will allow you to match the color of a fabric or other material if samples aren't available.

- Color in the furniture items on the floor plan when purchased; for example, when the sofa is purchased, take a colored pen and fill in the sofa's outline. This method will provide an easy visual record of what's been purchased and works especially well for large projects.

- Create room-by-room binders containing all samples, furniture photographs, paint colors, wallpaper samples, etc. Even photographs of area rugs, lighting and other items in the room are helpful. The more complete the better!

- Create a room-by-room spreadsheet with an inventory of what you already own and items you want to purchase. This allows you to sort by category when you go shopping. It is also a helpful way to track all items from selection through delivery.

- After ordering items, keep the purchase order (or receipt) in your folder so you can track the progress of the transactions (a spreadsheet would be handy here as well).

- Keep all receipts for future reference. Receipts can be given directly to an insurance broker to determine the worth of a household's contents, or they can be used later to order additional items from the same line or manufacturer. You may also need them to document the cost of your home improvements for tax purposes (the cost of improvements may be added to the cost basis of your residence when it comes time to sell).

Groupings of personal items—vases, bowls, globes—help give large homes a sense of human scale. Designed by Benjamin Noriega-Ortiz.

TEAM SPIRIT

By their nature, large projects add an additional layer of complexity. Large home specialist Andrew Goldstein, named the Builder of the Year for 2003 by *Custom Builder Magazine*, is well versed in the difficulties of custom construction. Though building any custom home is a challenge, says Goldstein, large homes have additional complications. "When a home becomes large—over 7,000 or 8,000 square feet—you cross a threshold," he explains. "You are trying to craft a very well-built, custom home, but you are beginning to move into systems that are normally used for commercial buildings. You have to somehow maintain that little jewel you are trying to build, yet you are working with commercial applications." To manage this delicate balance Goldstein advises putting in the extra effort to assemble the best team you can find.

All of the projects in this book were created with the help of at least one design professional. More often than not, it took a team of professionals to create a single successful design project. Inescapably, design and construction are team activities. Many individuals and firms come together on a specific site to collaborate. "You learn that in this field you must work with other professionals, and you pool or share knowledge to be successful," explains Howard Chezar. This combining of forces not only happens between the general contractor and his subcontractors; it starts at the top, and works its way down.

"Everyone from the architect to the plumber looks to the owner for direction, if not literally, then in terms of motivation. You want the owner to introduce the element of cooperation and camaraderie." Chezar says that common courtesies such as ordering pizza for lunch, or giving small gifts at Christmas, go a long way towards boosting morale:

"These small gestures are a terrific investment, as they inspire the subcontractors to care about the project."

Most design professionals encourage the owner to get involved with the project. In fact, avid owner participation often leads to the most successful projects. The strength of the relationship between the owner and

A large project can involve many professionals, from architects to art installers. Designed by Harriette Levine.

INSIDE
FENG SHUI

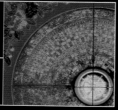

BY BENJAMIN HUNTINGTON

FENG SHUI PRIMER

In the simplest terms, Feng Shui can be described as a 5,000-year-old Chinese art that reveals the hidden links between ourselves and our home/work environments. It enables us to rearrange anything within any space to achieve a greater harmony and balance in all areas of our lives as well as enhance and support our personal ambitions and dreams.

Some of the basic tools used in Feng Shui are as follows:

■ Tao: Our instinctual connection to nature.

■ Yin/Yang: The integral balance of all things.

■ Chi: The way all of the energies interact with one another and the surrounding space as well as the five elements; it is the substance, connection and control between everything in our world.

One of the more complex tools of Feng Shui is the Ba Gua—a map that, when aligned correctly within any space, reveals the instinctual connections between parts of the physical space and the various parts of our emotional life.

The particular style of Feng Shui presented in this book is a unique personal blend of traditional Feng Shui methods and learning with contemporary scientific and psychological discoveries, an understanding of cultural anthropology and current design techniques. See subsequent chapters for specific tips.

professional, whether it is the architect, interior designer, general contractor or landscape designer, is the key element in keeping the project on track. Residential architect Ran Oron says the success of a project depends on several factors, but the most important is the chemistry between client and architect. "The sensibilities should match—fields of interest and mutual backgrounds are important."

A strong collaboration between owner and professional fosters a highly personal and successful project. Chezar recalls one client who was an artist. "She spent several days working side-by-side with the tile contractor, painting messages and designs on the backs of glass tiles, and helping place them. The finished product was a one-of-a-kind room to her exact specifications." Chezar says not every architect, contractor or subcontractor can handle this level of owner involvement, but there are professionals out there who appreciate it. "I welcome that kind of enthusiasm. I want the owner to be a part of the collaboration. It's a wonderful way for the client to realize their vision."

Every homeowner is different. Some are very well versed in the methods and means of construction, while others have never picked up a hammer. You are the best judge of how much you should contribute to your project, based on your skills and experiences. If more experienced, you may choose to undertake many of the project's tasks, hiring only the occasional consultant to perform specific assignments; however, if you are less experienced, you may want to opt out, leaving the bulk of the work to the professionals. Whatever your comfort level, when hiring any design professional take care to select ones that are both professionally competent and temperamentally compatible, because work on a large home will take place over an extended period of time.

By working closely with your design professional, you can incorporate items that are important to you—such as this homeowner's collection of chinoiserie—into the overall design. Designed by Noel Jeffrey.

A love of books was worked into the architecture of this room—creating built-in bookcases turned this living room into a library. Designed by Ilemeau et cie.

By working closely with an architect from the beginning, you may be able to affect where things like light switches are placed so you can avoid interrupting a blank wall you intended for art. Designed by Margaret Wetzel.

The design professional's role does not end with the planning stage, which encompasses discussing and identifying specific solutions and then rendering them in two dimensions. It goes right on through to construction and installation. Construction is a messy, chaotic process that can be anxiety-producing. Architects and designers can oversee and manage the entire construction process, supervising all aspects of a remodeling or redecorating job.

Having a trained professional who has been through the ordeal countless times before can be very reassuring. With literally hundreds of decisions to be made, it is comforting to have the expertise of a professional to help you overcome the challenges of a potentially large and imposing project. To find an expert in your area, turn to *Appendix: Resources* to see a listing of top design associations; most of these offer an online directory of accredited professionals.

CLOCKWISE FROM UPPER LEFT Whether it's building cabinetry, painting rich hues, decorating with pattern or selecting and displaying accessories in a unique fashion, design professionals can handle all aspects of customizing a large space. Designed by (clockwise from upper left) Virginia M. Witbeck, Ed Russell, Greg Jordan and Robert B. Green III.

> ## "There are few things more satisfying than a successful project." — DAVID HAVILAND

SPEND A PENNY, SAVE A DOLLAR

Regardless of size, any project takes a lot of coordination and thoroughness. On most of his projects, classically trained architect Peter Pennoyer cooperates with mill workers, electricians, engineers, interior designers, landscape architects and lighting designers. He stresses the benefits of bringing the team together for the initial design phases. "You need to coordinate the architecture with the engineering, so you don't have functional elements ruin your design. Know where the ductwork is going, and where the electrical outlets need to be, etc." Pennoyer admits that it is often tempting to avoid hiring another professional: "It's another fee. And you're thinking, 'This project is already complicated enough!' But bringing in professionals who know their trade early in the design process can actually save you money in the long run."

Garden designer, author and co-host of TV's *Surprise by Design* Rebecca Cole emphatically believes in the benefits of early expert advice. "You should definitely hire an expert, if for no other reason than to advise you in the beginning. A local landscape designer will know how to avoid the usual mistakes. He will have tried all the plants in your area before, and knows what will grow and what won't. Think of all the expense you can save by not planting a garden that might die in a month or two!"

The same can be said for architects and designers. In the process of developing sketches, elevations, floor plans and mock-ups, architects and designers take the guesswork out of the design process. Pennoyer talks about the confidence that mock-ups, or samples, can provide. "Although they aren't specific to big spaces, mock-ups are certainly vitally important when specifying miles of molding for a large house. Rather than design it and tell the contractor to build it, we commission a sample of, say, two feet

20 QUESTIONS TO ASK YOUR ARCHITECT

1. What does the architect see as important issues or considerations in your project? What are the challenges of the project?
2. How will the architect approach your project?
3. How will the architect gather information about your needs, goals, etc.?
4. How will the architect establish priorities and make decisions?
5. Who from the architecture firm will you be dealing with directly? Is that the same person who will be designing the project? Who will be designing your project?
6. How interested is the architect in this project?
7. How busy is the architect?
8. What sets this architect apart from the rest?
9. How does the architect establish fees?
10. What would the architect expect the fee to be for this project?
11. What are the steps in the design process?
12. How does the architect organize the process?
13. What does the architect expect you to provide?
14. What is the architect's design philosophy?
15. What is the architect's experience/track record with cost estimating?
16. What will the architect show you along the way to explain the project? Will you see models, drawings, or computer animations?
17. If the scope of the project changes later in the project, will there be additional fees? How will these fees be justified?
18. What services does the architect provide during construction?
19. How disruptive will construction be? How long does the architect expect it to take to complete your project?
20. Does the architect have a list of past clients that you can contact?

Reprinted with permission from the American Institute of Architects (AIA).

of a cornice molding. The owner can see it, we can make sure it's done correctly, then the builder can produce it without worrying that it might be wrong."

Interior decorator Lee Cavanaugh of the Manhattan-based firm Cullman & Kravis adds, "By doing floor plans and detailed measurements ahead of time, we are able to make sure a piece of furniture will fit in a room, or through the front door." Cullman & Kravis designers have had to solve many problems when homeowners, who were unaware of hidden pitfalls, purchased items on their own. "We've come to the rescue with all sorts of solutions like hiring an upholsterer to remove sofa legs and backs, just to be able to get the piece into the apartment."

COST ANALYSIS

If you're not careful, one large space can be more costly to build than the same amount of square footage in multiple small spaces. Peter Pennoyer explains, "When you have one space with 20-foot ceilings, the project is bound to cost more than a project that has two rooms with 10-foot ceilings. The reason starts with scale—all of the architectural elements need to be enlarged to be legible in a double-height space. Take the crown moldings—they would need to be more than double in volume than the moldings of two normal-height rooms. It's basic mathematics. If you take a drawing that is one foot by two feet and double it, you're quadrupling the area of it. Architecture has a similar impact."

Scale leads to other cost considerations, such as available materials and additional labor. Building materials that are sold off-the-shelf are typically manufactured for standard-sized spaces (eight- or nine-foot ceilings), which means if your space is larger, you may need to specify custom goods, or combine readily available materials.

SEEK AND YOU SHALL FIND

Finding the right professional to handle your job does not have to be difficult. To make the selection process easier, and to make an informed choice, follow these key guidelines:

Interview more than one firm; most homeowners consider between three and five professionals for each job.

Find potential candidates through personal referrals, industry associations or design media.

Start with the established businesses in your area. References will be local and easy to check.

Hire your main design professional, such as the architect or interior designer, first—he or she will be able to refer other tradespeople (though the final decision will be yours).

When interviewing, ask about education, training, experience, professional affiliations and credentials.

Ask about past projects; it is important to hire someone who has done work similar to what you have in mind.

Call all references; try to see some past projects.

Discuss all fee structures—most professionals have a variety of billing arrangements—and find one that works for you.

Coordinate with all tradespeople early in the process—it makes for harmony between landscape and architecture. Designed by Dick Clark Architects.

Custom molding and woodwork can add up—consider combining regular moldings to make unique combinations. Designed by Jeffrey Bilhuber.

Also, handling these larger-than-normal materials requires special care. Pennoyer cautions that normal ladders will not suffice on a project with high ceilings; therefore, scaffolding and other staging may need to be factored into the cost of labor. To navigate these murky waters, again, turn to the professionals. Architects are specifically trained to create solutions while considering costs, making choices that will provide the most value for your investment.

GOING TO CONTRACT

When you have envisioned your project, answered all of the design questions and found the right professional for

Rather than specify costly moldings in this large space with high ceilings, the architect created archways to add visual interest. Designed by BBG Architects.

the job, it is important to get all of the details into a contract (an exercise that will take place with each and every professional hired). Contracts are essential documents that serve to define the scope of the project, and the deliverables of the respective parties involved. All requirements and expectations should be mapped out, including what is to be built or designed, who will perform the tasks described, where the construction will take place, the level of quality, the schedule, the date of completion, and the budget and fee structure. This formal agreement is an opportunity to make sure everyone involved in the project is on the same page. Before signing, review all documents thoroughly, making sure all details are included and accurate. A well-

In this modern space, the ceiling was treated with girders and cross beams in a dark color, which adds both interest and visual weight—keeping ceilings from appearing out of scale. Designed by Sidnam Petrone Gartner.

executed contract will protect the homeowner in the end. For sample documents contact the American Institute of Architects (AIA). (Their information is listed in the appendix.) Since 1880, the organization has provided standard forms of agreement for use in the architectural and construction industries.

Sometimes it is difficult, if not impossible, to get answers to all of your questions at the outset of a project. If that's the case, it is often possible to hire design professionals on an hourly basis for consultation. Most architects, landscape designers and interior designers are available for pre-design services; they can help you determine the scope of the project, including lead-times, and cost of materials and services. After the project becomes more defined, it may make sense to shift compensation structures from hourly to another cost basis such as a percentage of construction costs, a flat fee or a fee based on square-footage.

JUMPING OFF POINT

There is a natural progression to the process of building or remodeling a home. By doing your research, mapping out your needs and desires and hiring the right professionals, you'll be well positioned to create your perfect home. Taking cues from the experience of experts will eliminate a lot of the guesswork and chance of mishap. By starting with the exterior of the house and working in, you can make your project flow smoothly, with room arrangements, furniture plans and lighting schemes coming together in concert. The following chapters, filled with colorful photographs and descriptive text, will help you flesh out your design specifics, and get you started down the path to completion.

Starting with a specific inspiration or theme, such as "Grecian bath," is the logical first step to creating a successful interior. Designed by Ike & Kligerman.

PUNCH LIST

- ☐ The design process starts with you. To create a house that reflects your needs and style requirements you'll need to ask yourself questions, and develop a game plan that the design professionals can follow.

- ☐ Asking questions about your lifestyle and budget constraints will help you determine the scope of the project.

- ☐ Regardless of style, budget or scope, the universal goal is to make every project livable, personal and individualized.

- ☐ To create a comfortable large room it is best to subdivide the space using either a decorative or architectural solution. For specific examples of design solutions, see the subsequent chapters.

- ☐ A visual library—a collection of photographs and tear sheets from various media sources—is an invaluable tool for figuring out and communicating your design likes and dislikes.

- ☐ Design and construction are team activities; many design professionals work together to create a finished project. Make sure to hire a competent and temperamentally compatible team, asking key questions and always working with a contract.

- ☐ A strong collaboration between owner and professional fosters a highly personal and successful outcome.

- ☐ You are the best judge of how much to contribute to your project, based on your skills and experience.

- ☐ In order to save money in the long run and avoid common mistakes, it is best to hire professionals at the outset of a project, at least for consultation.

- ☐ When budgeting expenses for a large project, keep in mind issues of scale, in terms of both materials and labor.

The approach to your home provides the first impression.
An entryway should be as appealing as the interiors within a
home. Designed by Peter Pennoyer; landscape by Madison
Cox.

CHAPTER 2

SITE & SCALE
CONNECTING THE LANDSCAPE

If you want to make your house feel "at home" in its setting, creating harmony between the interior and exterior environments is a necessity. The approach to your home will make the first impression, and regardless of how effectively

you have achieved intimacy within the interior rooms, if your home's surroundings aren't appealing, the overall impression will be less than welcoming. How your home is located on its plot and the landscaping used around it are critical when its profile rises resolutely toward the sky, because a large home will seem out of place on a parcel of land that contains minute natural or architectural features.

"One of the things that makes a large house successful," remarks Boston architect Thomas Catalano, "is a sensitive response to the context. We try and look at the architectural character of the surroundings. If there is an existing set of buildings around which you can draw some inspiration from and react to, that's important. Also, a home's success has a lot to do with the landscape. If a large home isn't sited in a sensitive way, it will seem even bigger than it really is." Though each of our experts echoed this sentiment, don't despair if you have inherited site-related challenges. You can learn proven tricks from the professionals to camouflage a poorly sited house.

THE A TEAM

The optimal team for creating a beautiful and comfortable home—whether the construction will involve a ground-up project or a remodel—includes an architect, an interior designer, a builder and a landscape designer. One of the strongest pieces of advice we've heard from our experts:

don't make your landscaping an afterthought. If you hope to create an overall feeling of intimacy, your home's surroundings should echo the style of the interiors. "These are not two separate worlds," says Greenwich, Connecticut,

The architecture of a house is more successful if it reflects the character of its surroundings and of neighboring buildings. Designed by Moore Ruble Yudell Architects.

> "I think how a house is sited is tremendously important. Before they build, I make sure that clients are aware of nature's influence on their property, such as the courses of the sun and the moon." — ZINA GLAZEBROOK

Situating a nook towards a natural view makes for an inviting place to sit. Designed by Glenn Gissler.

interior designer Alicia Ritts Orrick. "When you build a house and you put in so much effort, you want to make sure you're seeing something beautiful when you look out the window."

A ROOM WITH A VIEW

If your home has an abundance of windows and you revel in the opportunity to live with the natural environment in constant view, living in a glass house will bring you a dramatically satisfying experience day after day. But if you value privacy, and you're contemplating whether walls of windows will fit your sensibilities, a site that provides little or no natural cover may not be the optimal choice. If you're building on property that hasn't yet been cleared, save as many sizable trees as possible, because towering trees will offer privacy and will create a connection between your home and the land. Rebecca Cole explains, "Many people clear the land, build, then hope to replace the trees. They've cleared a sixty-year-old forest and they hope it will grow back, but it will never look right." Though you may incur additional costs when you ask your contractor to navigate around a smattering of trees, experts say the rewards are commensurate.

If you're building a home with copious windows on a site that's been partially cleared, situate the large rooms with expanses of glass toward any natural screens that still exist. Manhattan architect Bill Petrone sited a home with a dramatic glass room between a hollow of rock and a copse of trees in order to make the outdoor spaces adjacent to the imposing room more comfortable for the homeowner. The site, which was treeless toward the street, terraced down to a wetlands area and a stand of trees in the back; the canopy of trees provided both privacy

and scale. "The room, which has ceilings that are 17 feet high, sits in a bowl of space," he explains. "The rock outcroppings and the house form an outdoor room on one side, which helps scale down what would normally have been a big open space; and an open space on the other side of the home was worked within the trees so that it forms another outdoor room. I don't think you could put this room on a street or in an open field in Kansas and make it work the same way."

A home with a view—and plenty of it—has become a valued possession, but some experts believe that living with nature in plain sight has its disadvantages, as an abundance of windows may lessen the beauty of the scene they expose over time. To illustrate this point, general contractor Howard Chezar tells a story about a friend who visited a wealthy master of the martial arts in Japan who had built a new home. Though it was perched on an extraordinary outcropping far above beautiful vistas, the rooms were oriented away from the views or only small windows framed the scenery beyond. "My friend, who was an architect, knew that the master was no idiot, but he couldn't figure it out," explains Chezar. "Then he was taken out to the garden for a tea ceremony, and there was an opportunity for him to stoop down and wash his hands in this little man-made stream. While he was washing his hands, he looked up and there was the view, accentuated by the shrubs and the rocks, but only from that humble position."

The story made a lasting impression on Chezar, one that he passes on to clients, as he believes it presents soulful wisdom. "When people have a great view, I find that more often than not they want to sock the living room or the master bedroom right in front of it—with huge windows, which say, 'Look at that view!'" he remarks.

TOP Natural cover—such as a copse of trees—outside a window will be valuable if you prefer privacy rather than view. Designed by Noel Jeffrey. BOTTOM This house, with its wall of windows, fits more comfortably into its setting because it was nestled into a bowl of rock. Designed by Sidnam Petrone Gartner.

Creating cover with vines on structures is a beautiful alternative to mature trees or architectural solutions. Designed by Barbara Israel.

"I've found that even great views lose their greatness if they're taken advantage of too much." To minimize the enormity of a view in your large room that overlooks a dramatic scene, Chezar recommends using divided windows, which break up the view. Though you will lose the windowed walls that will fully expose nature's every mood, you will gain privacy and appreciation. Orienting your home so that only certain rooms take full advantage of the views will achieve a similar restraint. "You can appreciate the view, but you humble it a bit," he says. "I think that can make the view all the more spectacular."

UNDER COVER

If you've found the home you've always dreamed you would own, and those glass-encased rooms are part of the package, there are things our experts suggest that will help you gain both privacy and the opportunity to live with nature in full view as the years progress. If your land is relatively bare, resist the urge to fill your property with small elements, even if your budget is limited. "Instead of buying twenty little items, just get one big tree that relates to the scale of your house now," advises Cole. "You don't want to wait twenty years for something to grow to the right size. That means for twenty years your house will look like it has the wrong size pants on."

Landscape designer Jay Archer recommends putting together a five-year plan right up front. Each phase of the plan should build upon your vision of a thriving landscape that will bring a welcoming feel to your home's setting. In the beginning, address needs rather than wishes. "Determine a hierarchy by asking, 'Is this a problem or is it a desire?'" he suggests. "If you have drainage issues, grading issues or safety issues, address those before you consider

the aesthetics; but keep in mind that there are ways to solve most problems that will enhance the aesthetics down the road. Everything that you do in landscaping and architecture should be functional, but if it works to the best result, it should also be aesthetically pleasing."

THE MARK OF MATURITY

If repair work necessitates the removal of plantings that have always seemed undersized in relation to your home's façade, this is the perfect time to test the theory that bigger is better. Landscape designer Eric Hagenbruch is always on

the lookout for mature tress and shrubs to add to his clients' properties. "One of the important reasons to find mature trees and shrubs is that when you plant them, they tend to make the property look as if it has been established for a longer period of time," he explains. "Making a home feel more established is a way to create a feeling of warmth, because the grounds will make the home feel as if it has been lived in and appreciated for a long time."

Hagenbruch notes that mature plantings are often removed from property that's being developed. As an example of an exciting find, he cites five-and-a-half-foot boxwoods that he located for a client's property. They were

Mature plantings add immediate character to a home's surroundings. Designed by Diane Durell.

Cutting steps into the grade of a hillside will create
architectural interest and provide added personality.
Designed by J. Robert Hillier and Barbara Hillier.

> "When there is only seven feet between the walkway and the foundation—which is what a builder will typically leave when constructing a home—it is difficult to landscape the area." — ERIC HAGENBRUCH

substantially larger than the stock that most nurseries carry, which are generally around two feet tall. If you see a piece of property that's being developed and the mature plantings are still in place, ask if they're for sale. These mature specimens could immediately bolster the scale of your landscaping in relation to your home.

Even if your home is situated on a very small piece of property, size still matters where landscaping elements are concerned. Cole favors evergreens because they grow quickly. She is especially fond of Cyprus trees because they echo the grace with which Italians welcome visitors into their villages. "In Italy, you see the vast pasture lands, then off in the distance you see these big, beautiful entryways to towns," she explains. "That's the way you have to think about your big, huge house and your little, tiny yard."

Choosing large plantings and trees in the beginning is especially important if landscaping plans will evolve slowly over time, because the fewer the details, the greater the impact. If you are just beginning your five-, ten- or fifteen-year plan, make several big, bold statements, as they'll hold their weight as the years go by. They'll also provide spots where smaller plants and architectural elements can be incorporated. Stepping down the scale—from your home's large expanse, to stately architectural and natural elements, to small flowers and adornments—is a formula to keep in mind as you try to create a compatible relationship between your large structure and everything that exists beyond its doors and windows.

Maples, elms and oaks are solid choices when stature is important. If you're not a tree lover or trees simply will not thrive on your grounds, planting vines on structures is a beautiful alternative, as they'll provide luxurious foliage and focal points to help right the scale of a large home on a bare lot. Hardy wisteria and prolific ivy weaving living mosaics around graceful pergolas or statuesque arbors will entwine your architectural elements with natural beauty.

MAKING THE GRADE

The ground is the starting point on which all of your efforts to improve your home's surroundings rest, and thoughtful grading of the landscape will help your home nestle more gracefully into its setting. "One little hill: it's amazing what that will do," remarks Cole. "Great grading can make a very large expanse seem more intimate."

If you have a hill near your home that's either out of scale or needs a bit of a makeover to enhance its personality, carving steps into it can right the scale and make the hill seem more appealing. If runoff patterns make cutting into the land unwise, large slabs of natural stone make beautiful steps and perfect backdrops for plantings. As with all landscaping elements, consider the scale of the steps, Cole advises, as small steps on a very large hill may be just as out of place as the hill itself. Creating one large step would be a better choice than carving steps that are too small. If small steps are entrenched in your landscape, creating undulating mounds of soil around the edges in a flowing pattern, then planting ground cover on the mounds will form natural sculptures. Flank the mounds with flowering trees, large shrubs and a sprinkling of perennial flowers to create a colorful pathway to and from a special spot.

TOO CLOSE FOR COMFORT

Experts insist that it's important to get to know your property before you decide where to place hardscapes (landscaping elements built with hard materials, such as

Keep the size of focal points on the exterior of your
home in mind. You wouldn't want a tiny deck punctuating
a large façade. Designed by JoAnne Kuehner.

concrete or wood) and constructed surfaces. "Ask yourself, do I want a patio here?" advises Cole. "Place your chair there and see how it feels." Archer warns that it isn't wise to place a patio or a deck too close to a large home, as sitting next to an imposing structure will greatly affect whether you feel comfortable lounging there. It may be wiser to insert transitional elements between patios and decks and a large structure. This will prevent feeling overwhelmed, and will create an inviting introduction to the outdoor rooms in which you will spend many contented hours during the balmier months of the year.

"If you construct planting beds and terraced gardens in the spaces where the land meets the foundation of your home, you will ease the transition of scale, and you will be surrounded by greenery when you step outside," explains Archer. "No one is going to stand right next to a very large building and be comfortable, so it's important to situate outdoor living spaces a greater distance from the house to create a transition of scale."

Because these spaces are often shrouded in shadow due to the expansive façade of a large home, plantings here will bring greater challenges. "Aesthetically, it can be particularly challenging to find plant material for so much shade while eliminating the feeling that you're dwarfed at the same time," explains Archer. "Before you decide what to plant in these traditionally shady spots, discuss what you are considering with a landscape or nursery specialist to see if the plants you are wanting to include will thrive in those conditions."

Hagenbruch advises anyone building a home to consider the area next to your home's foundation early in the design process. "When there is only seven feet between the walkway and the foundation—which is what a builder will typically leave when constructing a

LARGE PLANTINGS THAT DO WELL IN SHADE

Shade-Tolerant Trees
Cercis canadensis (Red Bud)
Cornus florida
 (Flowering Dogwood)
Tsuga canadensis (Hemlock)
Ilex opaca
 (American Holly)—grows large
Ilex meservae
 (Blue and China Hybrids)—
 stays small

Shade-Tolerant Shrubs
Amelanchier
 (Shad)—the size of a small tree
Hamamelis (Witch-Hazel)
Kalmia (Mountain Laurel)
Myrica (Bayberry)
Pieris (Andromeda)
Thuja (Arborvitae)
Viccinium (Blueberry)
Ilex crenata (Japanese Holly)
Ilex glabra (Inkberry)

Perennials
Alchemilla (Lady's Mantle)
Astilbe (False Spirea)
Hemerocallis (Daylily)
Heuchera (Coral Bells)
Lobelia (Cardinal Flower)
Monarda (Bee Balm)

Trees That Will Tolerate Moderate Shade
Acer japonicum (Japanese Maple)
Cornus kousa (Kousa Dogwood)
Magnolia virginiana
 (Sweetbay Magnolia)

Shrubs That Will Tolerate Moderate Shade
Vibernum tomentosum
 (Double Fire Vibernum)
Rhytidophyllum
 (Leather Leaf Vibernum)
Dentatum (Arrowood Vibernum)
Calycanthus floridus
 (Sweet Shrub)
Fothergilla Gardenii (Fothergilla)
Aronia melanocarpa
 (Black Chokeberry)

Provided by landscape designer Bill Meyer

Before installing hardscapes, try placing a chair or a bench in a particular spot and sitting there during the time of day you'll spend out-of-doors; this will insure that your choices bring enjoyment, not disappointment.

A covered porch is a wonderful transition between house and landscape—the roof provides a comfortable sense of scale. Designed by Cynthia Lloyd-Butler.

> "Situate outdoor living spaces a greater distance from the house to create a transition of scale." — JAY ARCHER

home—it is difficult to landscape the area," he explains. "If I am involved in a project from the start, I have them leave 15 to 20 feet." The extra room allows Hagenbruch to layer plantings. "The larger the bed, the more interest you can build," he says. In the background of large beds, Hagenbruch will often plant flowering trees. Next, he'll add rhododendron, and then flowering shrubs. Finally, he'll use an assortment of perennials and annuals to complete the composition. If you've inherited a home where the sidewalks simply do not leave ample room for large plantings or layering, this could also be the perfect spot for a sculpture.

STEP IT UP TO STEP IT DOWN

Think about architectural elements that could help relieve the scale of your home's imposing façade. One sizable article with presence—a great statue or an antique Adirondack chair nestled in a bank of flowering trees: anything that makes a statement—will make your home feel as beautifully furnished outside as it is inside. Cole says you should look for items that excite you and then echo the colors of these pleasing objects in your plantings. "If you find a white antique iron bench that inspires you," says Cole, "put spirea in front of your house instead of boxwood. If you start with an inspiration like that and use it as a starting point to beautify one area, it will lead to other areas through repetition of elements."

Before creating focal points that will add character to your outdoor rooms, Hagenbruch says, you should become familiar with every corner of your property, not just the portion of it that's closest to your home. "Walk the property to get a feel for the landscape," he says. "Then create focal points that draw the eye. If you have a small tree

INSIDE
FENG SHUI

BY BENJAMIN HUNTINGTON

ORIENTATION WITH FENG SHUI

Ideal and Difficult House Positioning: House B represents ideal positioning on a hillside. House A is too exposed, while C is in shadow and dwarfed by the mountain.

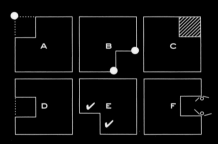

Missing Areas of a House: Often, we inherit a house footprint that is not "whole," and Feng Shui can help balance what's missing. In A, the missing section represents power; to compensate, place something substantial—a boulder, tree or bush. In B, compassion is lacking; compensate by placing a pair of objects in each corner. In C, relationships suffer; cure this by building a deck or patio, or adding gravel. D lacks community; seal the gap by building a fence or planting a linear row of bushes. E is missing wisdom; compensate by placing a mirror in either of the missing corners. In F, creativity is missing, so shine a light on the subject with outdoor light fixtures.

WAYS TO USE STONE IN THE GARDEN

Fieldstone
Paths, stone walls and veneer

Quartzite
Irregular paving and veneer

Granite
Steps and abstract garden
sculpture when chunks are
turned upright

Bluestone
Stepping-stone paths or
irregularly set patios

Crab Orchard Stone
Walkways, pool areas and veneer

Limestone
Walkways, terraces and
dry-stacked retaining walls
(use sparingly in damp
climates, as limestone
is porous)

Take a bird's-eye view of your property into consideration
before planning your landscaping elements. Designed by
Chris Becker.

that's in the distance, place a bench beside it and create a stone path leading to it so that the path draws you to that area." Keep in mind the size of these focal points, advises Cole. "You can't have a little walkway and a big house; you have to have a grand entryway," she remarks. "So even if you think, 'Wouldn't it be pretty to have a perennial garden,' if it's a big house in a big yard, a perennial garden probably is not how you should plant the front of your house."

A BIRD'S-EYE VIEW

If the area surrounding the foundation of your home is not the ideal spot for the nodding blooms that summer's warmth will bring, look to other areas on your property where plantings can be introduced. In order to facilitate your planning, Cole says to consider your property from an aerial perspective and think of all of the elements in your yard as architectural elements, including the house and the driveway. Planting beds or trees are also elements in the composition. If the driveway is off to one side of your property, you'll want to balance its large mass with an equally substantial mass somewhere on the other side of your plot. This could be the perfect spot to create a planting bed that will initially contain shrubs and flowering bushes. Over time—as the bushes mature and grow taller—plant medium and small plantings around them. This could also be a wonderful spot for a beautiful statue or a garden bench.

Very often large homes are placed far from the road, so what's planted at the entrance to your property should echo the landscaping closer to home. Cole suggests you think of your entire property as you would an interior room, and—again—think big and bold to echo

the stature of your home. "Take some of the elements used near the house and repeat them," says Cole. "You wouldn't just have an orange couch and not repeat that color anywhere else in a room in your home—you would include something else orange, such as an orange lamp, in the room."

THE FOUR SEASONS

There's an added challenge in landscaping which is less of an influence on interior design—the seasonal factor. When it comes to thriving in any kind of weather, not all plantings are created equal. As an example of the care required when beautifying a home's grounds during all four seasons, Cole cites the homeowner who plants a rose garden at the entrance to a home for the cottage feel the flowers

evoke and the pleasant aroma they yield. But, because the roses will not bloom during the colder months, the entryway is flanked by what amount to small, dead shrubs for much of the year unless the home is in a temperate climate. "Subsequently," remarks Cole, "the house looks like no one lives there—it looks like a haunted house!"

Hagenbruch follows a proven formula that creates texture and beauty, especially important when the plantings flank a home's entry. "I usually layer with trees—possibly evergreens—and then spot some perennials and some annuals in the area," he explains. "I also use flowering shrubs, such as rhododendron and azaleas." Though Hagenbruch points out that these amenable shrubs are being used repeatedly in landscaping, it's because they're some of the best solutions to providing evergreen coverage in the winter and flowers in the spring.

When adding buildings to your property, remember that the better they reflect the style of the other buildings, the more at home they will appear. Designed by John Rodgers, Inc.

If your home is in an urban environment, see that your outdoor spaces blend with the surroundings. Use materials such as brick that are reflected in the cityscape to create a more harmonious space. Designed by Paul Silverman.

> "Take some of the elements used near the house and repeat them. You wouldn't just have an orange couch and not repeat that color anywhere else in the room." — REBECCA COLE

STYLE CONSCIOUSNESS

When architects and landscape designers approach projects, respecting the past is an important consideration if a home has a history. Your home will project the proper charm if the inside and outside have been designed to work in concert stylistically, especially if a particular historical period is evoked by the original structure or structures on your property. If you'll be expanding your home, Pennoyer says, there are times when slight variations on a theme will enhance your home's exterior more brilliantly than a strict adherence to period aesthetics. "If a home looks too big, it's usually because it's too much of one thing," he explains. "You don't want to make the whole thing look like it was done at one time if you have a plausible story for why the house looks the way it does." Imagine a large, rambling farmhouse, he says, and the farmer who owned it. At one point, suggests Pennoyer, he came into money and decided to build a ballroom for his daughter's wedding. Then the daughter moved in, so he built a new wing for the grandchildren. Each new addition carried a slightly different feel, though the architectural styles did not clash when combined.

To illustrate a successful architectural ruse, Pennoyer describes a Virginia pool house that echoes the style of one of the farm buildings on the property. "We designed it to look like it had been a farmhouse, which had been turned into a pool house in 1924," he explains. "It looked like a renovation of an older building, even though the whole thing was new." Because the style of the farm buildings on the property was mimicked, a greater cohesiveness was created between all of the property's elements.

What's good for the buildings is good for the gardens, as a garden—formal or informal—should also reflect the period and style of the buildings on your property. Barbara Israel, whose book *Antique Garden Ornament: Two Centuries of American Taste* is a leading source guide for identifying garden artifacts, explains: "When we see a statue in a garden that's beautifully placed in an old-fashioned, classical way—the way an Italian statue would be placed in a garden—we have a visceral response to that which says, 'That's the way it's supposed to look.' When things are well placed in a garden—just as we thoughtfully place antiques in our interiors—we show that we respect history."

Though modern interiors support a sprinkling of traditional accents out of doors, creating a thoroughly modern garden to complement a quintessentially traditional house will create discord between the interior and exterior environments. "If you've gone totally traditional inside, and you go wildly modern outside, I don't think it would work," stresses Cole. "I think there has to be elements of both things inside and out." Israel agrees. "If you have a contemporary house, you should have an informal garden," she explains. "In very simplistic terms, an informal garden is one that is engineered to look like nature. It might have rustic forms in it or faux bois benches. You might have serpentine pathways or something stark, like a single urn or a Japanese lantern."

The formal garden, which enhances many traditional architectural styles, explains Israel, will most likely be geometric in form, and will include elements such as cross axes and straight paths. Statues in formal gardens are historically placed at the intersections of these pathways. This is especially true if the garden graces a large home on an expansive estate. "If it's a grand garden, boxwood hedges could form part of the architecture," she explains. "This would lead your eye to the statue that's nestled in the midst of them." If you've purchased property with a formal garden that has fallen into disrepair, and you plan to restore it to its original

splendor, Israel recommends that you do your research. It will make all the difference in ensuring that the garden and its many elements feel authentic.

WATER, PLEASE

Fountains and birdbaths are two elements that Israel believes will beckon people into the garden for the pleasure they offer. She also favors them because they create a connection to nature. Jay Archer agrees. "It's exciting to have water in a landscaped environment because it's a living element," he explains. "It has a life of its own, and it adds sound and depth. Fountains are also great ways to affect the transition of scale." This is true because fountains, as do any substantial architectural structures, provide height and mass. Placed strategically, they step

Planting a wall of climbing vines brings nature right up to the house in this country setting.

down the scale of elements in front of a structure, and create backdrops for plantings and smaller accents.

COUNTRY HOUSE/CITY HOUSE

Though most urban havens lack large expanses of green and long, winding driveways, the same rules apply. If you live in an urban area and your outdoor room consists of a petite terrace, Cole advises against filling it with small accents. "The reason it seems tiny is because everything around it is too big," she explains. "Put big things on the tiny terrace and then it will seem like it fits with the rest of the environment." Another important consideration: make sure your city home's surroundings blend with the larger urban setting. "If it's an urban environment, you should be using urban materials," explains Cole. "If there is no other wood to

A large statement—a tented room—makes a small terrace in New York feel more in scale with the surrounding rooftops. Designed by Vicente Wolf Associates.

Create private sanctuaries in your landscaping for personal escapes. Designed by Cynthia DiAngelo/Site Effects.

be seen around the city, I don't think you should use it." This means you should pay special attention to what you're seeing from the terrace. If your view encompasses black tar, steel and rusted metal, those are the materials that will bring agreement between your outdoor spaces and the setting in which they reside. This is where you'll get to be very creative and bring your own vision to an outdoor space, which will complement your unique interior.

THE SECRET GARDEN

Though a large home demands heavy-hitting landscaping solutions, don't forget to afford yourself some delicious privacy by creating intimate places to which you can escape on those long, lazy afternoons when the air is balmy and the shade is a welcome companion. "It is nice—especially in large spaces—to have little, secret areas, too," says Cole. "Long vistas may hold a big beautiful urn, which you approach down a garden path. Create an area off to the side that you don't see until you're beside the urn that will serve as a private sanctuary."

Give your home a comforting outdoor presence, says designer Zina Glazebrook, and you will appreciate the effort every time you come home. "Carefully consider everything about how you approach your home," she says. "How do you get to the house? How does it feel when you are walking in the door? Do you want to sit in a particular spot in the afternoon because you're going to capture a beautiful sunset? Do you want a balcony off your bedroom to make it easier to reach the stream or the swimming pool?" The more thoughtfully you consider how the exterior of your home will influence the look and feel you hope to achieve in the interiors, the easier it will be to create a comforting and beautiful home inside and out.

PUNCH LIST

☐ **Do not make landscaping an afterthought.**

☐ **Create a five-year plan, beginning with a comprehensive wish list. Ask your landscape architect to price each phase separately, and if the entire plan is unachievable all at once, prioritize and work toward the plan's completion over time.**

☐ **Situate large, heavily glassed rooms toward natural screens, such as trees.**

☐ **Buy larger-scaled landscaping elements to match the size of a large home.**

☐ **Undulating grades will make a larger home appear more "at home" on a site.**

☐ **Choose landscaping elements that inspire, and then repeat the colors of those elements throughout the property in plantings.**

☐ **Match a home's landscaping to its architectural style.**

☐ **Natural elements, such as water, in a garden create a soothing effect.**

☐ **Layer plantings next to your home: start with a flowering tree closest to the foundation, then plant rhododendron. Next, flowering shrubs add more color, and finally, a mix of perennials and annuals complete the textured composition.**

☐ **Echo surrounding materials, such as brick and metal, if your outdoor space is located in an urban environment.**

☐ **Don't forget to incorporate private garden areas on a large property.**

The flow from one room to another and within substantially sized rooms is a critical early consideration when the large home is being planned. Designed by Brooks & Orrick.

CHAPTER 3

CRAFTING THE PLAN
DEFINING SPACE BY FUNCTION

Planning for a large home is not remarkably different from planning for a small home in terms of trying to create functional rooms that flow gracefully from one to the other. In both cases, the job of the architect and interior designer is to

understand how you will use the rooms before the planning begins. Lifestyle and daily routines are important considerations, as is the vision you hold for how you want your home to feel. Architect Monique Corbat-Brooks remarks that the early planning phase involves more than a little juggling between the elevations and the furniture plan. Being flexible up front will insure that the circulation within the rooms of your home and the flow between them are accommodating and efficient. "It has been our experience that if you focus only on the outside, it's impossible to really make a plan flow correctly all the way inside," says Corbat-Brooks.

Regardless of the size of the rooms, the hierarchy and relationship of each of them to the others—or the flow of your floor plan—will create a unified environment if thoughtfully considered. The function of each of the rooms is the number one factor in determining which rooms should be placed side by side. Interior designer David Easton remarks that the flow of rooms within a home is similar to music. If the rooms work well together, there is harmony. If not, a floor plan will jar the sensibilities the same way a grating musical composition will. This is especially true when one space functions as several rooms.

FIND THE HEART OF EVERY ROOM

Corbat-Brooks and her partner, interior designer Alicia Ritts Orrick, believe that every room has a heart; if you find it or create it, you'll introduce intimacy every time. "When we look at a room," explains Corbat-Brooks, "we try to discover its heart; it's not just a space you're walking through that doesn't relate to anything else. Each space has to work to create a strong sense of place

Find the "heart" of every room. Even natural sunlight filtering through a window can create an intimate focal point. Designed by Brooks & Orrick.

within the home." The heart of a room comes in many forms, adds Ritts Orrick: "Whether it's a fireplace or the built-in cabinetry in the library or the sunlight that is coming into the room, these are important elements. The only rooms that really work are the ones that people spend time in."

Manhattan interior designer Katie Ridder concurs, adding that many successful rooms have more than one purpose. "An example that comes to mind is Jackie Onassis' apartment on Fifth Avenue—her dining room was book-filled: library during the day, dining room by night," she remarks. "Even if you have a large, large house, it makes it feel cozier to have more than one function within each room. I'm thinking of our house, which can be cold and drafty, and the nicest place to be is in front of the fireplace, so you want to be able to do a variety of things, all in front of the fireplace." This was true of Onassis' apartment, she adds, explaining, "Her fireplace in her library looked like the nicest place. You want to read there during the day and eat there at night, then curl up there after dinner. If you have a big, sprawling space, you'll find yourself gravitating toward whatever place is the coziest."

KNOW THYSELF

Identifying these cozy spots and defining ways to introduce them into all of the rooms in your home is the first step to assuring that you'll create pleasant, livable spaces. Architect Thomas Catalano remarks that there is always a logical flow that emerges from the client's lifestyle and preferences. Zina Glazebrook agrees: "With regards to the flow of rooms, you have to define your priorities. Maybe the homeowner wants a really big library with a fireplace because they are avid readers. Maybe it should be near the

kitchen because they love to have small meals next to the fireplace. I believe that you can be very clever and design houses that speak to people's needs."

The rooms that are the easiest to make comfortable are usually the kitchen and the family room because these are the most lived-in rooms. Rooms are always defined by purpose, and some rooms are defined by the activities that are carried out in them—sleeping, bathing, reading, working, eating, entertaining or cooking a meal. These rooms offer lessons that you can use to make your entire home more useful and personal. Sometimes introducing a special activity in even the least lived-in rooms will bring you and your family back to the space time and time again.

Create a flow in your rooms that makes sense for your lifestyle. This will make your home feel more comfortable as you go about your daily routines. Designed by Carl Steele Associates.

Built-in cabinetry can lend a room character, drawing you into the space again and again for quiet relaxation. Designed by Sidnam Petrone Gartner.

"With regard to the flow of rooms, you have to define your priorities." — ZINA GLAZEBROOK

In task-oriented rooms like kitchens and bathrooms, it is easier to define the functions and design accordingly.

"I think the rooms that are the most difficult to make intimate are living rooms," remarks Ritts Orrick. "I think the biggest mistake is that people don't design these rooms to be truly lived in. To make a living room livable, you need a television, computer or place to listen to music: you need the things that draw you there." This is important advice if you've envisioned your living room as a wonderful place to entertain but nothing else. If this is the room's only purpose, it will likely remain empty most of the time. Create not only seating areas that will make the room a wonderful spot for entertaining (interior designer Matthew Patrick Smyth recommends no more than eight people in one area to allow for comfortable conversation—see Chapter 6, *Decorating Details*, for more information), but also include a game table where children can play Chinese checkers or adults can gather to play cards. Desks are also versatile furnishings to include in a living room. Place one near the fireplace, and you'll have a wonderful place to use your laptop when you're home alone; then use it as a buffet for a casual party.

Greenwich architect Jay Haverson and his wife, Carolyn, who is a graphic designer, designed a main living space that is a large, open room. Several sitting areas—one by the fireplace and one that's focused around a television—segue into a dining area and a spot where the couple have a partner desk. Because the room is used for a variety of different purposes, they spend many hours there participating in activities that are specific to the four cozy spaces within the larger space.

Another example of a room that serves several purposes is one designed by New York interior designer Benjamin Noriega-Ortiz. He incorporated a desk into the design scheme of a 20-foot by 20-foot master bedroom in a Miami Beach home. "My client wanted his desk right next

to the bed because that's where he wanted to check email," says Noriega-Ortiz. "This wasn't because of a lack of space, but because of function."

A desk was also the desired addition in a Park Avenue apartment Noriega-Ortiz designed. "We cut the dining room into thirds, and used one third for an office," he explains, "delineating the space with columns, so that the room remained open." Though he would normally advise against putting an office in a dining room because it's challenging to keep a desk neat, this particular client is extremely fastidious. In the office portion of the room, a television cabinet, desk, credenza and a table holding a

Adding a desk to the living room creates a reason to use the space. It can double as a serving table when entertaining. Designed by Joanne DePalma Design.

lamp serve double duty when guests are welcomed. "If they are entertaining," explains Noriega-Ortiz, "they clear the desk, turn the table and use the surface as a buffet or as a bar. It is a strange pairing, but it actually works really well."

GO WITH THE FLOW

Space-savvy architect Glenn Leitch agrees wholeheartedly that a room should have multiple purposes. He also believes that early in the game clients focus too much on how a home should look, and not on how they want their spaces to accommodate their lifestyle. Leitch says it's hard work to keep clients focused on how their rooms should be optimally arranged, but it's worth the effort. "I give my

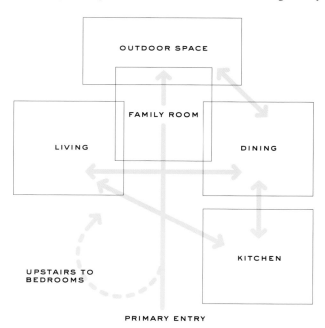

OUTDOOR SPACE

FAMILY ROOM

LIVING

DINING

KITCHEN

UPSTAIRS TO BEDROOMS

PRIMARY ENTRY

Architect Glenn Leitch, AIA, suggests his clients draw bubble diagrams such as this one to demonstrate how they move between rooms. The diagrams will eventually turn into the finished floor plan.

clients an exercise: to create a bubble diagram that shows how they want the rooms to flow and where they want their furniture," explains the fan of diagramming. "I then do a simple sketch to see how their ideas play out." Once this phase is completed, Leitch talks with them about how they want the home to feel, but only after the plans are coming together. "At that point," he adds, "they are really involved in the process."

Questions such as "Where do you spend most of your time?" and "Do you cook often?" are asked. "Sometimes people will say, 'No, I don't cook, but I still want a big kitchen,'" he says. "I think it's good to get people involved in the process in this way because they usually get what they want if they are." Diagramming to problem-solve a floor plan and room layout will help you create a more cohesive plan, even if you're flying solo, without the host of professionals who are normally involved in the process. "Most people want to be picking out their windows and the stone for their countertops right off the bat! But I say to clients, you have to go through this hard work because you will have a home that satisfies you if you do," says Leitch.

HOME IS WHERE THE HEARTH IS

"I think the kitchen is the heart of the house," says Glazebrook, "because it is a really important room for comfort." Though the large home often contains a sizable kitchen, Glazebrook cautions against making the room one large expanse if cozy areas of respite are missing. "I believe a kitchen should be intimate at all costs," she explains. "If you are planning a large kitchen, create small areas, such as a great little desk or a wonderful dark leather banquette with a table tucked in a corner of the

OPPOSITE Before building, it's important to think about how you will move through the space. Do you like extended hallways? If so, how can you make the most of these transitional spaces? Designed by Eddie Jones, Jones Studio.

room. This will bring the scale down and make the room seem cozy."

The kitchen is one area, say experts, where personal preferences are extremely important. Even if you do not cook, you'll likely spend time in the kitchen with family and friends: that quick cup of coffee shared before dashing out the door in the morning, and the glass of wine poured together at the end of the day are special moments shared with loved ones. To make a kitchen feel more like a room you'll want to spend time in, give it warm, homey touches. Rather than covering a large island with stone—which has become so popular—Glazebrook prefers using wood, as it will make the island seem table-like. She also prefers islands that incorporate seating, as the area will become a spot for friends and family to gather when a meal is being prepared. Thoughtful areas like this will bring large rewards, but they'll also add space to the room, as the kitchen is one of the busiest rooms in the home. As the room expands to allow for traffic that's likely to ebb and flow, it will make it easier to identify corners where smaller seating areas can be placed or a nook near a sunny window where a desk will offer the perfect spot for writing letters while you're having tea in the afternoon.

Interior designer Miles Redd remarks that the kitchen is more commonly the domain of the architect than any other space in the home. "If I am in a meeting where the kitchen is being designed, I bring up points of practicality," he says. "I ask my clients, 'Do you really need a big kitchen?' In New York, the answer is often no because people mostly order take-out or dine out." In these cases, Redd will recommend that the kitchen be made smaller and the captured space be used for a playroom or a laundry room—spaces that will add to the quality of life of the home's occupants.

In a large kitchen, it is important to create cozy areas like this breakfast space. Designed by Cullman & Kravis.

QUESTIONS TO ANSWER BEFORE CREATING A HOME PLAN

- Are you single or will you be sharing the home with a partner?

- If you are married, do you have children?

- Do you spend a great deal of time at home, or very little? (This could determine the size and arrangements of your rooms: if you come home late from work after dinner at a restaurant, you might want to have your bedroom close to the kitchen so you can grab a quick glass of wine before you head to bed to watch the news or read the newspaper.)

- If you spend a lot of time at home, what rooms do you prefer to spend time in?

- Do you like to cook? (Do you both like to cook?)

- Do you like to entertain at home?

- What hours of the day do you spend at home? (This could determine whether you want a library off the master bedroom that faces the direction of the sun for your morning hours with coffee or whether a sunroom that catches the evening rays in the summer is more important.)

- This two-dimensional planning is the most important part of any design process, says Glenn Leitch. "This determines how the spaces go together, how they work for the homeowner. The architectural plan then becomes a three-dimensional piece, but if the process works properly, the important considerations are solved in the two-dimensional phase." Be certain to address your day-to-day rituals in the diagram phase, adds Leitch, as determining these rituals will help you make your home a personal haven. And remember to think creatively. "If you have a very large kitchen, it can actually be a couple of rooms in one," he says. "You could have seating in a portion of the room where you have a TV and a couch. Then it becomes a space that you can actually live in. On paper it really may be this giant kitchen, but it is actually a kitchen and a den."

A thoughtfully designed kitchen is a pleasure for the cook and for the guests who will be drawn to the kitchen while meals are being prepared. Designed by Sidnam Petrone Gartner.

For clients who do like to cook, Redd says bigger can be great, citing the kitchen he designed for a client who wanted a dramatic and fully functioning kitchen. "We decided to put some big elements in it, like a ten-burner stove," he explains. "There is one enormous counter space for prep work. Though the kitchen is large, it is actually fairly compact, because a highly functional kitchen requires that you have everything within arm's reach: you don't want to walk ten feet every time you need a spatula!"

Benjamin Noriega-Ortiz advises you to think carefully about how you want your kitchen to function before you decide where the elements will go. "If the client is going to do a lot of baking, then you have to design their kitchen so that they don't have to pass through the space where another function is being carried out," he explains. "You would want to set the room up so that the cooking is being done in one area, the baking in another, and service is being performed in the third." This is important because constant interruptions are a frustration when meals are being prepared. Though these different tasks require different areas, Noriega-Ortiz recommends making everything compact, or the size of the kitchen may become overwhelming.

Kitchen designers understand the concept that a cook should be able to grasp any item needed for any task by reaching out. If you're designing a kitchen on your own, this is an important point to keep in mind. The ideal kitchen, say experts, is organized into specific areas: a baking center, a food preparation center and a clean-up center. The questions that designers will ask to help you configure the unique kitchen that will suit your needs range from "How do you cook?" and "How do you entertain; do you use caterers for large or small parties?" to "Do you have children?"

Even the largest kitchen can be made to function like a dream if planned properly. Designed by Sidnam Petrone Gartner.

Design your kitchen to suit your needs and it will be a room you'll enjoy being in even when meals are not being prepared. Designed by Benjamin Noriega-Ortiz.

Though the "work triangle" in the kitchen has been greatly modified since it was first articulated in 1949, the logic is still solid: keep the appliances and the features that you use most often as close at hand as possible. The National Kitchen and Bath Association publishes guidelines for traffic and workflow that will benefit you as you plan your beautiful new kitchen.

MIX IT UP

Kitchens have few passive spots, but other rooms will contain a mix of passive and task-oriented areas. Asking whether a spot in a multi-functional room is a passive one—such as a corner where a large sculpture will be displayed—or one that will be focused on a particular task—such as watching television, sitting in front of a fire, listening to music or reading—will help you determine where you will spend time in a large room. The question will also help you decide how to group seating arrangements to allow for ease of circulation. This is very important, remarks Haverson, because when you're placing objects in a room, you have to imagine how you'll move around in the room. "You're going to have points of focus, and these are going to be the places you'll want to be in the room; that's what makes a room," he says.

Sometimes a room is both a focal point of the home and a pathway to another room. Glazebrook designed an East Hampton home where the living room was virtually a hallway that spanned from the entryway to a library. "The room is really a rather grand hallway, so the furniture couldn't protrude very far into the room," she explains. "We based everything around the fireplace and kept the ends of the room open, just as you would in a hallway. I placed what I call static furniture there—a trunk

Ask whether areas in a room are passive ones or task-oriented ones. This will create an obvious logic for your furniture plan. Designed by Thomas Catalano, AIA.

INSIDE
FENG SHUI

BY BENJAMIN HUNTINGTON

LIVING SPACES

The principles of Feng Shui offer important solutions to allowing energy to flow freely and positively in an interior. Many of the precepts are nature-inspired and each of them will help to foster comfort for the human being in his or her environment. Below are suggestions for bringing tranquility into prominent areas of your home.

ENTRY AREA

Make sure that sure the door opens easily (this provides a welcome "open door" to all).

Hang something inviting on the wall to the right of the door (as you enter), e.g., a picture of a wide landscape or happy home, a mirror (to reflect your visitors) or a table with a bowl on it (a place to put things).

Identify the area of entry with an area carpet, lighting or a different color.

Provide a view or directional indicator into the heart of the home, e.g., a large horizontally rectangular depth view on the wall opposite the door, a table placed to guide people into the space or repeater icons (lamps, colors or images) leading inward.

LIVING ROOM

Make sure that the seating in this room stands on an area carpet (this will help to unify the seating group).

Provide a focal point in the space (this will unite the people using this area).

Vary the lighting around the perimeter of the room (this mimics an environment that is closer to what we find comfortable in nature).

Limit views out of the space with the use of curtains, screens or furniture placement (to prevent focus outside of the space, and to provide a safe and comfortable area).

BEDROOM

Select softer furnishings (to identify tranquil use of space).

Place a strong image above the head of the bed, e.g., a picture of mountains, earth-toned fabrics, or a square picture, not a depth view, of a solid-looking object (this will provide "mountain" energy to define the wall behind your head when you sleep).

STANDARD MEASUREMENTS FOR FLOW PATTERNS

- The distance between people in a seating group should not exceed 10 feet.
- Doors and openings in major traffic ways should be 36 inches wide.
- A space of 42 inches should be maintained between a buffet and the chair of the closest person seated at a dining room table for ease of serving.
- A passageway of 38 inches should be maintained between the walls in a dining room and the dining room table and chairs for ease of passage and chair movement.
- An opening of at least 12 inches should be left between any wall and a bed.
- A 42-inch pathway should be maintained between the bed and a closet for dressing activities.

at one end and a pretty little chair at the other. It could be pulled up, but it was truly only there as a decorative object. I also included some very interesting artwork."

With circulation in mind, furniture plans may need to be fine-tuned several times. This is where you decide between putting that statuesque armoire in the spot where you imagined it would create a dramatic focal point, or leaving the space open for children to race when they're playing with friends. There's always logic to a room that will be defined by the special circumstances of yourself and your family. Once you've identified the floor plan that makes the most sense for everyone who'll live in your home, you can use the formulas that architects and interior designers use to determine whether enough space is left between furnishings and groupings to allow for easy passage.

Flanking a hallway with shelves for books creates a transitional space between rooms while adding great aesthetic value. Designed by Michael Graves.

If designed thoughtfully, a beautiful home is more than a set of design decisions: it's a reflection of the homeowner's dreams. Designed by Brooks & Orrick.

> "It's not so important that you tell an architect how you want something to look, but to describe your aspirations for the space and let him interpret it and come up with ideas to show you." — JEFFREY COLE

THE END OF THE TRAIL?

Not only do you want to be able to move around in each room with ease, you want your rooms to flow from one to the other gracefully. The kitchen, living room, dining room, library and screened porch are rooms that are generally built around lifestyle, remarks Haverson, so when planning how to situate these rooms, ask yourself how you'll get from one to the other, and whether you'll want to go directly from certain rooms into others for particular reasons. Also ask yourself if the room is at the end of the trail or if it's a stop on the way.

"If it's the most important room in the house, it's going to be the end of the road," he explains. "It will be the one you're going to want to show your most special guests and friends, or it will be the room to which you will retire at the end of the day." Whether it is formal or informal is not a critical determination at first, he adds, but planning the most important room so that the other most lived-in rooms are convenient to it is. To insure that your most important rooms are at the center of your home, you will need to articulate how you live, and then communicate how you want your rooms to work for you if you are hiring professionals.

In an Idaho residence designed by architect Coty Sidnam, the clients had particular requests for the master bedroom suite. They wanted to strike a balance between entertaining—as they'd likely have a lot of company—and maintaining their privacy.

Though the clients did not say in initial meetings that they wanted to include a library and a study in the suite, they were clear that they didn't want to have to make business calls while sitting on the bed, and they wanted to be able to watch television in private when guests were visiting. To satisfy these requests, a library in the master suite doubles as a television room. Sidnam also placed cabinetry for a television in the master bedroom, allowing husband and wife to watch television separately without leaving the suite. "They also have a bathroom, a powder room and a study," says Sidnam, "so they can lock the doors to the suite and have everything but the kitchen at their disposal."

The desires of Sidnam's clients were thoughtfully considered because they were able to convey their habits and temperaments to the architect. "It's the aspirations of the clients that the architect has to interpret," says Manhattan architect Jeffrey Cole. "It's not so important that you tell an architect how you want something to look, but to describe your aspirations for the space and let him interpret it and come up with ideas to show you. More than, 'I want the kitchen here and the living room here,' I try to listen to my clients' desires for their lives, and then figure out the best way to create a layout."

GIVE IT A BREAK

When there are a number of extremely large rooms in a home, Catalano says, transitions can help bring the scale down to a more manageable level. Citing a Weston, Massachusetts, home that he designed, which contains towering main rooms, he explains how spaces tucked into the floor plan added cozy transitions. "There is a logical flow from the stair hall/reception area into the formal rooms: the living room, dining room, study," he says. "The study and the living room back up to each other, and they are both expansive rooms, so we filled a space between them with a fully enclosed bar. It's designed so that you walk into the bar from either the living room or the study. Even though the composition of the very large home is somewhat picturesque, it's important that we maintain a strong sense of symmetry and proportion between the

Is a room the end of the trail or a stop along the way?
Creating a bathroom that is relaxing will make it a prized
destination at the beginning and end of every day.
Designed by Brooks & Orrick.

PUNCH LIST

☐ Create furniture plans first to identify areas where circulation could be inhibited.

☐ Identify the "heart" of every room and make it your focal point and the basis for your design in that room. If you're building a home, make sure you create a heart for every room.

☐ If you will be hiring professionals to design your home, allow them to get to know you and your family. It will be the personal touches that he or she includes in the design process that will create intimacy.

☐ Rather than creating a large living room that will serve primarily as a place to entertain, include task-oriented areas—such as places to read, to use the computer or to play cards—so that the room becomes one that you and your family will be inspired to use even when guests are not visiting.

☐ Rooms should flow harmoniously from one to another.

☐ Kitchens are rooms that demand a high level of functioning, but they don't have to be cold and institutional. Make your kitchen warm and inviting by adding cozy spots that will draw you and your family.

☐ Determine whether a room is the end of the trail or a stop on the way.

☐ Don't be distracted by the visual elements of the interior design phase until you have finalized the floor plan and furniture plan or you'll run the risk of creating an aesthetically beautiful home that doesn't suit your needs.

☐ A sprinkling of cozy spots will turn a large, open floor plan into a series of bold, beautiful spaces intertwined with intimate, delightful ones.

larger rooms and the other, smaller spaces." This smaller space relieves the grandeur of the large rooms and provides a welcome respite.

Given the many solutions our experts have presented, it's clear that there are as many ways to make a home suitable for a person, couple or family as there are experts. A keen and fully articulated awareness of your lifestyle and full participation in the planning phase of the building or remodeling of your home are important tools in planning an environment that will bring you hours, days and years of satisfaction.

Creating cozy spaces between substantial rooms is a way to make a large home feel more comfortable and intimate. Designed by Noel Jeffrey.

The open floor plan of this home allows unobstructed views from front to back, but the partitions with glass insets can be drawn closed to create separate rooms. Designed by Sidnam Petrone Gartner.

CHAPTER 4

ARCHITECTURAL SOLUTIONS
IF YOU BUILD IT, YOU'LL HAVE WON

The experts all agree that to create a comfortable, livable large home, you need to find ways to delineate space. "To make a large room cozy, you have to define the space, whether that's using architectural elements like arches, or

alternating the materials," explains general contractor Howard Chezar. "You want to modulate the architecture so that you are enticed by spaces," adds interior designer David Easton. This is something architects do every day by designing physical separations, using planes, vertical walls, horizontal ceilings and floors and decorative applied moldings as fundamental elements. "You have to first find out what emotion you want to convey," says Easton, "then you can gain that particular emotion with architectural detail."

DEFINING SPACE

"I am fairly traditional, in that I prefer rooms to just open spaces," says architect Peter Pennoyer. "I generally think that defining rooms results in more usable space." Rooms are made up of three major surfaces: walls, floors and ceilings. There are many ways to work with these surfaces to define space: You can build walls, partitions or architectural screens; you can vary the floor level, texture, finish or pattern; you can lower ceiling heights with dropped soffits, decorative beams or other types of adornment; or you can use moldings to horizontally divide unmanageably large planes. Whatever architectural method you choose, the end result should be to separate your space into manageable living areas. As Pennoyer puts it, "Architectural articulation, even though it may mean giving up a little bit of square footage, usually makes the space feel better."

Moldings, such as this wainscotting, can effectively divide a wall, creating a more comfortable sense of scale. Designed by Victoria Hagan.

THE FLOOR BENEATH YOUR FEET

"Start with the floor—it's a great place to add decoration—and work up," says interior designer Katie Ridder. Many architects and designers echo this sentiment, believing that the floor plan or footprint of a property will dictate the feel of the entire space. "The way you address the floor will set the tone of the interior," says designer Miles Redd. "The shape, pattern and materials will all make a difference."

While walls may be the most visible surfaces of a room, floors are the most tactile. The choice of material will make a strong statement in your home. There are plenty of options to choose from, including natural materials such as stone and wood, and man-made materials such as tile, linoleum and carpeting. Stone, selected and installed properly, can be incredibly durable and timeless. It is a rich material that provides an elegant, affluent look. The main drawback to using stone is cost. Since it is a natural material, there are limited supplies, and the weight makes shipping and labor costly. The other potential disadvantage is that stone is a hard and sometimes cold material; if not tempered, these characteristics could translate to the interior as a whole. Tiles can also appear hard and imper-sonal, especially if they are highly glazed. But unlike stone, they come in an infinite number of colors, and can be warmed up with various shades. For example, terra cotta tiles, originating in the Mediterranean, automatically bring a sense of warmth to an interior. Since they do have such a strong geographical affiliation, though, make sure that these particular tiles work well with the style of your house.

In between hard and soft floor materials, you'll find wood and resilient flooring. Wood is another versatile material that works effectively in large spaces; as flooring, it has infinite variations, such as wide or narrow planks, parquet or herringbone patterns, stained or bleached, hard or soft, inlaid with central medallions or rosettes. Once considered a low-end product, resilient flooring, such as linoleum, vinyl, cork and rubber, has evolved a great deal and now comes in many different styles, some elegant, some practical. It's a cost-effective alternative, and you can get most resilient flooring materials in sheet or tile form, for added flexibility.

Technically, carpeting is not an architectural solution, though because it may be the fastest and easiest way to cozy up a large interior, it's worth mentioning as a flooring solution. A very versatile product, carpeting is made of natural or synthetic fibers, comes tufted, knotted, braided, hooked or woven, and can be solid or patterned. (For more on carpeting, see Chapter 6, *Decorating Details*.)

Large expanses of floor offer wonderful opportunities to do bold patterns. Inspired by the elaborate interiors of European palaces, interior designer Bunny Williams designed a parquet de Versailles floor in the lavishly formal foyer of a Manhattan residence. As Redd, who worked with Williams on the project, recalls, "You definitely couldn't have had that large, complicated herringbone floor in a smaller space. You needed the scale of that room—its width and length—to get it to read properly."

CHARACTERISTICS OF FLOORING MATERIALS

Ceramic Tile: **Cool, manmade, colorful**

Concrete: **High-tech, polished, smooth, hard**

Polished Stone (e.g. marble, granite): **Refined, cool, durable, formal**

Porous Stone (e.g. limestone): **Old world, less formal, warmer**

Resilient Flooring (linoleum, vinyl): **Sensible, low maintenance, inexpensive**

Terra cotta Tiles: **Warm, Mediterranean, friendly**

Wood: **Flexible, timeless, natural**

OPPOSITE Stone is an exceptional floor treatment, but if not tempered with warmer materials, such as these richly stained baseboards and woven area rugs, it tends to make an interior feel cold and impersonal. Designed by Moore Ruble Yudell Architects.

THE GREAT WALL

Walls in spaces of any size are large and obvious. They serve important primary functions as construction elements, boundaries of space and functional portals. They also represent a great opportunity to create compelling, personalized environments.

At its most basic, the purpose of a wall is to indicate a change in space. And in any structure, the placement and arrangement of walls will affect your movement, gently directing the flow or circulation through the building. In addition to creating reactions and influencing movement, the placement and arrangement of walls within a space sig-

nificantly influence a structure's internal composition and the harmony of the whole. Like a rest in music or a line in a painting, architectural space gains meaning through composition and delineation—achieved, essentially, through the use and positioning of walls.

Traditionally a wall needed, at the very least, to support itself. However, when walls serve as partitions to delineate space, and are not required to bear loads or offer structural support, the constraints evaporate. For example, when designing a "wall" or partition using fabric, anything goes. (For more on fabric walls, see Chapter 6, *Decorating*

Curved walls can make a room feel cozier, with furnishings cradled within the circumference. Outside it, the curve helps move people through the space. Designed by Jeffrey Cole.

Details.) For the contemporary designer, the possibilities are enormously rich and varied.

When freed of the requirement of holding up weight, walls can be made of virtually any material and in any shape. For example, in a New York apartment, Redd created a clover-shaped dining room with gracefully curved walls. Redd decided on the unconventionally rounded walls for functional reasons. "The clients wanted the ability to seat twenty-five people when they entertained, yet they also wanted to dine alone in the same room." The clover shape provided the perfect solution, as the mammoth rectangular dining table fit in the central east/west axis of the room, while a smaller, circular table nestled into one of the north/south clovers. "The curved walls cradled the smaller table, giving a sense of coziness," says Redd. When guests were not present, four could dine at the small table without feeling dwarfed by the room and the massive table; and when festivities were in full swing, the small table doubled as a dessert buffet.

This freedom enables walls to be utilitarian, or act as armatures for decorative displays of art or books. In a loft space, interior designer Thomas Jayne designed wall partitions that are essentially free-floating bookcases that do not reach the ceiling. This kept the integrity of the open floor plan, while providing a sense of enclosure. Chezar also thinks creatively when building walls, looking for ways to add interest and function without changing the basic architectural layout. In a long hallway, he decided to add visual interest by puncturing the walls with architectural niches. "They varied in size and depth, breaking up the long walls with indentations, which were lit suitably for displaying artwork," he says. "Some were deeper and meant for sculpture, others were shallow and designed for paintings."

Designer Benjamin Noriega-Ortiz also uses walls to great effect. In past projects, he has created a wide variety of partitions using all sorts of materials such as fabric, wood, metal and traditional sheetrock. Often these "walls" are unconventionally shaped, fall short of full height and/or are movable. In one project he created a low, wrap-around wall to shelter two chairs that floated in the middle of a vast living room on axis to the entry. "I built the wall to make a clean entrance—you don't want to enter a room and see the back of two chairs—and to protect the people sitting in them," he says. "Nobody likes to be surprised from behind."

When walls, like Noriega-Ortiz's, are impermanent, the layout of the room becomes much more flexible. While the basic characteristics of the room remain the same, the introduction and removal of folding screens and sliding panels or doors can re-create and redefine the space whenever desired.

When walls are non-structural, architects can create a wide variety of options, including decorative partitions made of unusual materials, such as this stained hardwood screen. Designed by Sidnam Petrone Gartner.

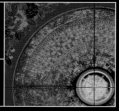

INSIDE
FENG SHUI

BY BENJAMIN HUNTINGTON

ARCHITECTURE

Feng Shui masters have long understood that rooms contain more than a collection of objects. How energy flows is always taken into consideration, and how emotions are influenced by a home's placement, the arrangement of its rooms, and its architecture and design are key considerations in the Feng Shui maxim.

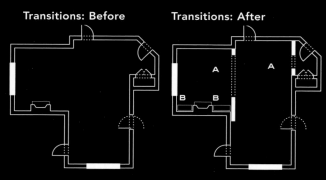

Transitions: Before   Transitions: After

Before: The original floor plan was laid out like a great room, with no architectural definition. It's just one open space, with no transitions.

After: By adding two arched openings (A), the space has been effectively divided into three spaces: library, living room and foyer. The spaces are still open one to the other, but with a sense of privacy and enclosure in each area. In addition, in the library area, bookcases (B) were added on either side of a fireplace to create a more defined focal point.

OVERHEAD

Architects believe there are certain opportunities that are only afforded by larger spaces. As Pennoyer says, "Large-scale rooms allow you to do very creative and amazing things, especially on the ceiling. With the greater distance and vantage point, you don't have to crane your neck to look at what's overhead." Trained as a classicist, Pennoyer tends to adorn all his ceilings in some way, whether it's a simple cornice molding or more elaborate paneling. In one San Francisco residence with 13-foot ceilings, he inset the paneling with tone-on-tone plaster bas-relief with natural motifs that included fish, animals and trees. "Something like that would look ridiculously busy in a small space," he says.

Easton believes that ceiling styles greatly affect the overall feel of a room. He gives an example of how architectural detailing choreographs the mood in a room. "Compare a tray ceiling—which rises and visually lifts the space in a room to create a feeling of expansiveness—to a low-slung ceiling—which evokes the sensory equivalent of walking into the taproom of an English tavern." The tray ceiling creates a feeling of openness, while the low-slung one creates a sheltered ambiance.

Curves in a ceiling, especially in a large room, help to bring a sense of gracefulness and togetherness to the space. Architect Jay Haverson explains why he feels a rounded ceiling has a wonderful effect on very spacious rooms: "What a vault does is collect things together. Because there's a low point and a high point, your eye tends to move from side to side, so it says that everything in the room is under one wing."

Staggering ceiling heights is another way to delineate space, and bring your eyes down in over-sized rooms. In a Sun Valley residence Coty Sidnam's clients wanted an open floor plan in the main portion of the home—which contained the kitchen, dining room and living room. To

OPPOSITE The design of the ceiling informs the overall character of a room. This tray ceiling sweeps up, creating a rising, open feeling. By painting it in a darker shade, the designer helped contain the ceiling, making for a cozier atmosphere. Designed by Jeffrey Bilhuber.

A darker or contrasting material helps add visual weight to otherwise lofty ceilings. Designed by Lake/Flato Architects.

achieve the openness her clients desired, yet still define the three different spaces, she varied the ceiling height over the dining room, creating the illusion of a distinct room, though there were actually no walls separating it from the other spaces. "The lowered ceiling helps it read as a separate room, creating a virtual delineation that makes the mind say, 'Aha: the dining room!'"

When you cannot change the shape of a room due to existing functional constraints, sometimes the most effective solution is to lower the ceiling. Architect Jeffrey Cole wanted to ground a transitional space in an Upper West Side loft, but because the ceilings in the home were concrete, he wasn't able to recess architectural elements above the ceiling plane. Determined to ground the space, he created a secondary ceiling, dropping it below the original one, and puncturing it with an oval soffit. "That was a very irregularly shaped room, which was carved out between the living room and the master bedroom," he explains. "There were step-backs on the exterior of the building that dictated how the room was shaped. You walk through the room at an angle to get to the master bedroom,

so the space was hard to define." He adds: "Curvilinear shapes punched into or cut out of ceilings in transitional areas can anchor rooms, making them more composed."

You don't necessarily have to lower the ceiling to create a cozier space. Using beams or coffers (open grid patterns created with beams or moldings on the ceiling plane) will help control scale and make a room more comfortable for the human figure. As architect Glenn Leitch explains, "Coffers define a space within a space. For instance, in a really large room, one coffer defines the living space, one defines the gaming area or seating within the living space, and another coffer defines the dining area. Even though it's all one space, the architectural demarcations divide the room into more intimate areas." In a project in Greenwich, Connecticut, Haverson used decorative beams on the living room ceiling, visually lowering it and creating more defined areas. "Breaking the room into smaller parts with the beams creates scale," says Haverson, adding that making bold statements in a large room should be done carefully. "The scale of a room could be ruined if the beams are too big, too deep, too thick or too light in color."

The beams on this ceiling visually lower the height, reducing the scale of the room to a comfortable level. Designed by Barbee Associates.

Moldings need to relate to your interior in terms of style and scale. In large rooms you need moldings with equal stature. Designed by David Easton.

ARCHITECTURAL DETAILS: MOLDINGS

The basic purpose of moldings, regardless of style, is to cover and embellish crucial intersections of a building, e.g. joints between the floor and the wall, ceiling and wall or opening and wall. The basic components of buildings can be broken down into two categories: surfaces and edges. Surfaces, such as walls and ceilings, are large, flat expanses of space that are fairly plain, and dominate the overall scheme of an interior; edges are smaller, secondary and more subtle—ranging from the intersection of two walls to the line where window and wall meet. Making the transition from surface to edge gracefully is where moldings come into play.

There are many factors to consider when choosing moldings, including style, balance and scale. Take the first factor: style. The use of moldings is traditionally associated with classical interiors. Perhaps it is the historic antecedents of the product—the highly ornamented Greek and Roman temples—or its subsequent overuse in various decadent periods, such as the Victorian era, that have soured some on the concept of moldings. Indeed, it can be quite easy to over-embellish, rendering an excessive or ostentatious interior through the use of inappropriate forms. In fact, mid century modern interiors generally are devoid of moldings. Walls meet windows and ceilings with a sharp border—no transition, just a hard line. Even today, many interiors are being designed without moldings, and in the right context, they can offer a space a crisp, clean quality.

If you do plan to incorporate moldings into your project, though, overall balance in an interior should be established by employing items of similar scale and weight. Consequently, there should be a direct correlation between the height of the room and the scale of the molding, whether it is a baseboard, casing or cornice. Builder Stephen P. Major writes about molding relativity in his book *Architectural Woodwork*: "The scale and alignment of crown molding should reflect the size and height of the room in which it is installed. Room height in particular affects perspective. Low ceilings cause the crown to be viewed more from the side than from below, so the profile should ideally extend downward more than outward. High ceilings change the perspective, and the crown should ideally be larger and project out onto the ceiling at least as much as it drops onto the wall."

The relative scale of various moldings in a room should be considered as well. It is important to have a harmonious transition between the different styles, thicknesses and widths within one room. Moldings come in literally hundreds of styles and sizes, available either as stock or custom orders. In addition, individual components can be built up and assembled to create a more elaborate, custom look. The task of choosing the most appropriate molding can be quite daunting. A helpful hint from the experts is to pick one design motif, such as egg and dart (molding with egg shapes alternating with dart shapes), or bead (narrow, half-round molding), and stick with it throughout the space. Or pick a highly decorative pattern for cornice molding, and then select simpler styles for coordinating baseboards, casings, chair rail and other accents. Designer Elissa Cullman recommends that you make slight adjustments in the molding from room-to-room: "In a very large house in Greenwich, Connecticut, we raised the wainscoting in certain areas, such as the breakfast room. Our reasoning was that in a large house like this there are so many circulation spaces, if the wainscot always stays the same height, the result is deadly."

In addition to harmonizing transitions, moldings can be applied directly to the wall surface to create an optical illusion of a lowered ceiling, or more proportionate walls. In a large living room in East Hampton, New York,

that had 12-foot-tall ceilings, Pennoyer built eight-foot-tall bookcases topped with decorative moldings that continued around the perimeter of the room, coordinating with doorways and arches. "In that room, the bookcases represent a typical wall height; the horizontal molding creates the division. The molding also works well with the architecture, becoming a springboard for the arched doorways." In a Concord, Massachusetts, home, architect Thomas Catalano did a similar thing in the living room, which had a rounded 19-foot, six-inch-tall ceiling. Because the ceiling was so tall, Catalano ran an entablature around the room to create a more comfortable scale. "We brought the apparent height of the ceiling down by running the entablature around the lower section of the room," he says. "This brought the

height down to people scale."

Though architectural detail of this sort creates a unifying effect in a room, it also offers practical timesaving opportunities. Sidnam elaborates. "Creating an artificial entablature or datum around the circumference of a room is a way to fast track a job, building any cabinetry before the rooms are actually finished," she says. "Because it's artificial, we don't have to worry about final dimensions. It's a way to design the home in a vacuum." She adds, "A big house takes a long time, so tricks like this can be important."

EVERYTHING IN PROPORTION

"In terms of scale, the classical rules of proportioning give you a good foundation to design a room or space, whether or not you're a classicist," says Pennoyer. Easton cautions against dividing a space by two. Don't use half the room for a seating area around the fireplace and half the room for a seating area around a set of windows, he explains; choose an A:B:A equation instead, such as a pattern of 8 feet: 20 feet: 8 feet. Dividing by one, three, five, seven or nine—as the Greeks knew to do—will result in a more balanced space. For instance, he continues, dividing a space by three and then adding pilasters is one way to make it more enticing. It's still a large space, but the columns give it a sense of division, therefore making it cozier. If you have a long room for a living room or a formal sunroom, break seating areas into unequal sections. Use one of the smaller sections at one end for an intimate reading area with chairs and a small sofa. Use the other smaller section for a grand piano or a game table. Then use the larger area in the center of the room for your main seating area where you will entertain guests. (For more on furniture arrangements, see Chapter 6, *Decorating Details*.)

ARCHITECTURAL TERMS

TRANSOM WINDOW: A window divided horizontally by a cross bar, or a window over a door, that is separated from the door by a transom (or cross bar).

ENTABLATURE: A beam that spans between columns, encircling a room well below the ceiling plane.

DADO: The lower part of a wall when adorned with moldings, or otherwise specifically decorated; an ornate wainscoting.

COVE/COVING: A curved surface forming a junction between a ceiling and a wall, e.g., a board that forms a shallow shelf that runs along the wall near where the ceiling intersects the wall (also referred to as a datum line).

COFFER: A panel deeply recessed into a ceiling created by the addition of crossed beams in a grid pattern.

OCULUS: A round window.

CLERESTORY: The walls that rise above a space containing a row of windows to admit as much light as possible (formally, in a Gothic church).

WAINSCOTING: Paneling that covers the bottom portion of a wall.

PREVIOUS PAGE A shallow shelf, or datum line, used near the ceiling in this bedroom ties the window and door trim to the custom cabinetry. It also allowed the cabinetry to be built before the room was fully constructed, as the cabinetry didn't reach the ceiling. Designed by Sidnam Petrone Gartner.

Building paneling that was as high as a typical wall (eight feet) made this tall space feel more proportionate. Designed by Peter Pennoyer.

OPENINGS: DOORS & WINDOWS

"It's a sensibility that has come to us from Vetruvius on down," says Easton, taking care to add that classical proportions are not always the answer. "How many times have we walked into a space that is classically correct, but it ain't exciting!" Architecture is an emotive thing, he concludes: "Modern or traditional—it should make you feel."

Doors are exceptional design opportunities—they can be customized more cost-effectively than many other design elements, and custom possibilities are endless. Designed by Michael Imber Architect.

Doors and windows serve aesthetic as well as functional roles. Doors act as entrances and exits, facilitating circulation. Windows bring in natural light and fresh air, as well as frame a particular view. Integral parts in the vertical surfaces of a room, doors and windows both offer an introduction or an embellishment to the overall style of the house, as well as an opportunity to add definition.

> "The play of light on glass can 'dematerialize' a space. It takes away the weight of the structure, making us feel we're somewhere between indoors and out. " — ELISE GEIGER

DOORS

"Doors have great design potential," says architect Elise Geiger, author of the upcoming book *The Essence of Home*, a look at seven essentials of home design. "They don't have to be the typical 6'-8" height, swinging from one side. A distinct proportion, a stained wood veneer, a pivoting, or even a beautiful decorative hinge can add character. Since they tend to cost less to customize than say, a wall of windows or a bank of cabinetry, custom doors can actually be a relatively inexpensive way to develop something individual in your home."

Other designers agree. Doors have the potential to be versatile, evocative and effective. Pennoyer cites an example of doors relating to the scale of the architecture in terms of both aesthetics and function. "At the Knickerbocker Club, there is a set of grand double doors on the inside of the library, but on the outside, in the hall, there is only one. Rather than widen the doorway to accommodate the double doors, they just added a false door in the stately room; this allowed them to keep the proportions right for both spaces." He adds, "You can actually be fairly imaginative, and be quasi-fictional in architecture."

Redd similarly used a set of doors to make a dramatic statement in the foyer of an important residence. "We mirrored a pair of antique wrought iron doors," he says. "It's just a big closet, but we needed a focal point." In the same residence, Redd used Tiffany's big platinum doors as an inspiration, and decided to add a metal inlay to all of the doors to public spaces. "We wanted references to the 18th century, and also the 1930s, but rather than do all metal, we choose wood with brass inlays," he says. "The space already had a lot of metal: a pair of Russian console tables, and large hanging light fixtures. The wood helped to warm up the space."

When confronted with a large open space, consider using pocket or sliding doors for a flexible solution. Chezar uses this typical Victorian solution to great effect in today's interiors. "In grand Victorian townhouses, they have those big sliding doors. If you think about it, it's the perfect solution. When you shut them, you have two very distinct rooms; when you open them, you have one large space."

Think about using glass doors in the interior. They will divide large rooms, yet still maintain an open feeling. Designed by Anthony Cochran.

WINDOWS

Some experts believe that the windows are the first thing people notice when they enter a room—nothing is more evocative than a room with walls of windows. Citing Philip Johnson's house in New Canaan, Connecticut, Easton explains that an optical illusion is created when the walls disappear, through the use of glass, essentially transforming them into landscape paintings.

As Geiger puts it, "The play of light on glass can 'dematerialize' a space. It takes away the weight of the structure, making us feel we're somewhere between indoors and out. To do that well, you have to pay attention to the quality of light, the proportions of glass to structure, the thickness of the glass, how the glass turns a corner, and how it meets the floor and ceiling planes."

Architect Bill Petrone also admires the room that invites the outdoors in through its windows. He says an abundance of windows is an excellent way to lessen the scale in a very large room. "The spaces that you see historically that are very massive and seem monumental are those spaces that are completely enclosed. They don't have a view of the outside to help moderate the scale," he explains. "If you're going to have a large space like that, a relationship with the outdoors is important. The view is changing all the time. This means you'll be reading something other than just a large room—what you're reading is how the light, sound, weather and seasons are playing on the space." In a monumentally large, glass-encased room in a home in the Hudson Valley, Petrone created a slight alteration with the window patterns. "We decided not to use a straight grid on the windows; instead we staggered them to match the irregular feel of the trees," he says. "This helped us achieve a closer connection to the site. Although it was a large space, we were trying to mimic—with very industrial materials—some of the phenomena that happened in the natural surroundings."

A view of nature helps provide a sense of scale to a room with double-height ceilings. Designed by Sidnam Petrone Gartner.

The circular shape in this ceiling helps direct the eye around the room, echoing the concentric pattern on the tile floor. Designed by Sidnam Petrone Gartner.

REPEAT AFTER ME

From the gridded expanse of glass to the play of patterns on walls, repeating shapes can effectively reduce the scale in a large room and bring symmetry to your design scheme. Sidnam says it's the consistency of the pattern that makes the scheme work in the large spaces. "I believe the worst failing a house can have is to try to be too many things at once," she explains. "For instance, to use every shape of window in the catalog; to walk into every room and have a different style—the French room and the Tudor room—doesn't make for a comfortable house. I think a place really starts to sing if it ties together." Sidnam put her theory into practice in a 10,000-square-foot, Craftsmen-style home in Sun Valley, Idaho. Throughout the entire project, she created compositions of squares and rectangles, echoing the patterns wherever she could: in moldings, wall panels, kitchen cabinets, light fixtures, stationary screens, window motifs and inset, camel-colored walls. The effect is a cohesive look that ties the whole house together.

In another project, Sidnam created a unified design in a bathroom by repeating a curved motif on the walls, ceiling, floor and fixtures. Her design culminated with an oval cutout in a dropped ceiling panel (made of stained wood), which she lowered below the original ceiling. Not only did the shape reaffirm the rounded wall, it also helped to direct the eye around the room, as did the concentric pattern in the tile floor. Had the only rounded shape in the bathroom been the wall behind the sink, the room still would have worked, but by echoing the curves with the ceiling cutout and the tile, Sidnam created visually exciting variations on a single theme.

If you're someone who prefers a bit of variation, experts say mix it up a bit. Citing a kitchen that he says seemed as if it went on forever, Noriega-Ortiz illustrates how subtle variations can create interest in rooms. "The

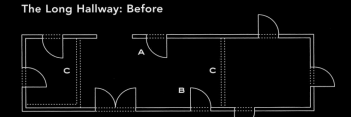

ARCHITECTURE CONTINUED

The Long Hallway: Before

The Long Hallway: After

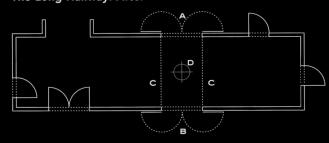

Before: In the original version of this long hallway, there were many doors opening at random; doors A and B, for example, don't line up, creating a lack of balance. There were also scattered beams (C) on the ceiling.

After: In the architectural solution, relocating the beams (C) to the center of the hallway and adding a central light fixture (D) creates a focal point and visually expands the width of the hall. The wider doorways (A and B) create a greater sense of openness and increased energy flow.

cabinetry was finished exactly like the floor," he explains. "It's oak with a greenish cast to it—it looks a bit like driftwood—and it unifies the whole kitchen, despite its many ins and outs." Though the color unifies, it could easily have become monotonous, so Noriega-Ortiz varied the treatments of the door-fronts. "The door is sometimes open, with glass, while other times it is closed." The unifying color gave the room its strength, and the patterning of the cabinet fronts created textural interest.

Sidnam used the same technique by adding dashes of glass to wood screens in a New York City townhouse. She inserted antique glass panes to help break up the monotony of the rectangular patterns that were repeated in wall paneling and floor-to-ceiling pocket doors. "If someone wants a lot of paneling in a room, and is showing me old English paneling, I can't just do the obvious," she

explains. "This is a modern space with very simple, very highly considered verticals and horizontals, so everything became long and narrow. It would have been wrong to use endless panels without varying them, because the rooms would have become monotonous repetitions of the same rectangular shapes in the same material."

MATERIALLY CONNECTED

Last, but certainly not least, choosing your materials is an important consideration, say experts. Materials go a long way towards setting the tone of an interior (think cozy carpeting versus cold concrete), and a change in materials or texture can indicate a change in space. For example, varying your floor materials in a large room will imply separate spaces. Chezar goes one step further, saying that

Using a calculated palette of materials, such as stucco, wood and rice paper, gives a cohesive, harmonious look to a project. Designed by Anthony Alofsin Architects.

the change in materials could be something as subtle as alternating the direction of the wood flooring.

Experts also caution against using too many materials in one space, which can make a room feel chaotic. As Zina Glazebrook puts it, "Everything has to work in concert; that's my firm belief. I always try to sell my clients on one group of materials. There's a very calming influence in using materials and repeating them throughout the outside and the inside of a project." Jeffrey Cole also strives to achieve a unified effect by controlling the materials in a project. "I try to use materials discretely," he says. "It's not a matter of how much or how little, but how well you are controlling the palette." Geiger adds: "Getting materials right is really about understanding rhythm and counterpoint. You need to find places to break from the palette in one or two places for contrast."

Adding antique glass panes to the sliding screens that divide space in this home helped to relieve the monotony of an abundance of wood. Designed by Sidnam Petrone Gartner.

PUNCH LIST

☐ Dividing large, open spaces with architectural solutions actually makes a room feel more comfortable.

☐ Start with the floor, and work your way up. Expansive floors offer a wonderful opportunity to make a statement with a wide variety of materials and patterns.

☐ Walls are the single biggest surface in a room— they are functional as well as aesthetic. They can be utilitarian or decorative. Designers use walls to divide and shape the feel of a space.

☐ Screens, bookcases and other flexible partitions are excellent ways to define spaces within one large room.

☐ Tall rooms offer an exceptional vantage point— make use of it by decorating the ceiling plane.

☐ Varied ceiling heights within one room will create the illusion of walls.

☐ Rooms are made up of surfaces and edges, moldings create harmonious transitions between the two.

☐ Take care to select moldings that reflect both the style and scale of the architecture.

☐ Doors and windows are excellent opportunities to extend the style of the room.

☐ Creating optical illusions with walls of windows is one way to give a sense of scale to large rooms.

☐ Divide large rooms by 3, 5, 7 or 9, never by 2. Choose an A:B:A equation, such as 8 feet: 20 feet: 8 feet.

☐ Repeated architectural details—if done thoughtfully—add interest to a room.

☐ Use materials discretely and repeat them throughout the interiors of your home to create a calming influence.

Working with decorative painters, the architect was able to interpret and expand the design of an antique architectural painting (located in the center relief with the light fixture) to fit its new location in a San Francisco townhouse. Designed by Peter Pennoyer and Katie Ridder.

CHAPTER 5

OPTICAL ILLUSIONS
THE MAGIC OF PAINT & WALLPAPER

Not every solution to a large space needs to be architectural. Countless experts have solved their design challenges using paint and wallcovering. There are distinct benefits to using these mediums, specifically flexibility, cost and time. Paint is

not only the most versatile and least expensive surface treatment available, but is also the one medium that offers an infinite range of possibilities. "To me it is all about paint," says New York City designer Thomas Jayne. "Paint is a great way to customize a space, using both color and texture."

One example of paint's prowess is the decorative finish. As an alternative to investing large amounts of money and time into custom moldings, natural stone or rare wood veneers, designers like Jayne often employ talented decorative painters to create the desired effect through the art of trompe l'oeil. The literal translation of trompe l'oeil is "to fool the eye." According to decorative painter Pierre Finkelstein, a graduate of the prestigious Van Der Kellen Superior Institute of Brussels and the winner of the Meilleur Ouvrier de France, the term trompe l'oeil means to create a three-dimensional illusion on a two-dimensional surface—for example, architectural elements such as moldings, pilasters, ornament, bas relief, etc. It can also mean to marbleize, create faux bois (wood grain) or paint grisaille (three-dimensional ornament with tone-on-tone decoration). These painted versions are considerably less expensive than the real thing, and take much less time to complete. Painters can come in and work their magic in as little as a few days, compared with the long lead times for manufacturing and custom installation of three-dimensional treatments. With an average lifespan of ten to fifteen years, a painted finish does not last as long as an

architectural solution, but it does have the advantage of being easily updated or changed.

Like paint, wallcovering is also multifaceted—it can accentuate the strong points of a room, while masking the weaker features. It can brighten a dark space, give definition to a room that has minimal architectural

In a tall room with very little existing architectural detail, wallpaper borders add definition to break up the large walls, while the dark green color on the ceiling brings it down visually to create a more intimate setting. Designed by Irvine & Fleming.

Color has a profound impact on the character of a space. This saturated orange complements the warm Southwestern theme. Designed by Jemison.

detail, or mask imperfections such as unevenly plastered or slightly damaged walls. According to the Wallcovering Association, "wallpaper is the great impersonator." Stripes and prints, for example, perform optical illusions that make rooms that look too long or too boxy appear more proportionate. Wallcovering—available in a wide variety of styles, patterns and colors—is practical and economical because it lasts seven to ten years, and can be easily replaced. With its many upsides, wallpaper can provide the perfect solution to a large space design challenge.

COLOR

Color, pattern and texture all affect the feel of a space, but without a doubt, color—especially on the walls—has the most profound impact. "Certainly, a white room is different than a red room in terms of enclosing space," explains David Easton.

Choice of color is critical. It can change the feeling of a space, as well as alter its perceived shape. The inherent characteristics of a color can either visually expand a room or envelop it, making it cozy and warm.

The range of possible color choices seems limitless. According to statistics, the human eye can register approximately seven million different colors. So the task of selecting the right one can be daunting. However, by understanding the fundamental components of color, and the ways in which various colors typically function, you'll be better equipped to handle the challenge.

All color is derived from three primary colors: red, blue and yellow. Each of these colors represents one third of the entire color spectrum. The traditional color wheel is composed of twelve colors: three primary colors (red, blue and yellow), three secondary colors (orange, green and

CHARACTERISTICS OF COLOR

Red: Powerful, stimulating, romantic, intense

Orange: Vibrant, dazzling, lustrous, youthful

Violet: Supple, otherworldly, smoky, rich

Yellow: Sun-drenched, radiant, luminescent

Blue: Soothing, aquatic, cool, icy, airy, sedate

Green: Spring-like, calming, botanical, relaxing, fresh, neutral

violet), and six tertiary colors (orange-red, orange-yellow, yellow-green, blue-green, blue-violet and red violet).

Colors are described as warm or cool, depending on their respective location on the color wheel. Reds, oranges and yellows are considered warm colors, reminiscent of the properties of fire: think candlelight or the sun. Blues, greens and violets are the cool colors, characteristic of the various shades of water. Just as these warm and cool colors elicit certain properties, so too do the rooms that are shaded in

Cool colors can be successfully used in large spaces, provided they are both dark and enveloping, or warmed up with contrasting painted trim, or used with light-colored furniture. Designed by Tonin MacCallum.

them. Rooms filled with warm colors feel cozier and closer, while rooms swathed in cool colors can seem chilly, distant and expansive. The colors and placement of the furniture and accessories in a room can either enhance or counter the warm or cool feeling created by the color of the walls. (See Chapter 6, *Decorating Details*, and Chapter 7, *The Right Stuff.*)

In addition to knowing about the color spectrum, it's helpful to be familiar with several color terms: hue, value and chroma. Hue is essentially another word for color; value is the lightness or darkness of a color; and chroma is the intensity of a color—how vivid or dull it is.

Color is dependent on light. When the eye registers color, it's actually seeing the light waves that have not been absorbed. For example, a typical green absorbs all of the red and violet light waves and reflects the green. The

To prevent monotony in a monochromatic scheme, add further definition to walls. For example, this green scheme, with both painted moldings of a more concentrated hue and a textured decorative painted inset, is anything but boring. Designed by Ilemeau et cie.

quality of light, whether it's natural or artificial, will alter the perceived color in a space. Natural light is particularly tricky, as it not only changes with the locale, the climate and the season, but also with the hour of the day. A warm climate, or a window that gets direct sunlight, will add a hot yellow-orange cast to your room, revving up any existing colors and making them seem warmer than they would on a cloudy day in a cool climate. With regard to artificial light, incandescent and halogen bulbs are warmer, giving off a yellowish cast similar to candlelight, while fluorescent light tends to have a bluish cast.

With all of these lighting variables, it's vitally important to make every color selection on site. The experts all recommend using mock-ups whenever possible, especially with paint, and viewing the samples over the course of several days under as many circumstances as possible. As color consultants and designers of architectural paint colors, Donald Kaufman and partner Taffy Dahl travel around the country, making site visits at all hours specifically to observe light changes. Kaufman explains, "This is not an exact science, there are no rules or automatic answers. Rather, it is a deliciously complex process. We study the space until it tells us what is needed, and then we create the exact hues that will enhance the space." Indeed, the complex interplay of color and light is so integral that Dahl and Kaufman recently published a book devoted to the subject, entitled *Color and Light: Luminous Atmospheres for Painted Rooms.*

Renowned designer Benjamin Noriega-Ortiz understands the effects of light on interiors, especially tropical light. Based in New York, but born and raised in Puerto Rico, Noriega-Ortiz works with many clients in Miami and Palm Beach. "There is so much natural light in Florida; it's wonderful, and I hate to cover it up," he says. "Plus, we want to enhance and embrace our location. Though dark colors definitely work to make a space feel smaller, I would never do that in Palm Beach. I tend to keep the color scheme light and harmonious, using other tricks to make the space intimate."

COLOR JUXTAPOSITION

The interaction of color in an interior also affects the feel of the space. A monotone or monochromatic color scheme (using a single color or similar values) will typically make a room feel larger, as there is no differentiation, no contrast. Kaufman says contrast is key in a large space. "The eye needs borders to delineate space—otherwise a tall room just looks taller." His advice for a large space is to paint

COLOR SCHEMES

Monotone: **single color with low chroma (e.g., all pale beige).**

Analogous: **the use of colors that are next to each other on the color wheel (e.g., yellow-green and green).**

Monochromatic: **single color, multiple values (e.g., many different shades of green).**

Complementary: **the pairing of colors diametrically opposed on the color wheel (e.g., green and red).**

Painting architectural details such as moldings, mantels and doors in a contrasting color, such as this bright yellow on dark blue, provides a framework for the walls and helps to contain a large room. Designed by Samuel Botero.

Color should be selected on site, with thought to the locale and the quality of natural light. Instead of using dark colors in this light-flooded bathroom, horizontal stripes in pale terra cotta and cream keep the high ceilings in scale. Designed by Stingray Hornsby.

moldings in contrasting colors, both in value and hue. For example, in a room with dark walls, paint the trim a light color. For further differentiation, choose complementary colors, such as pale yellow trim on dark blue walls. "If you handle your trim in this fashion, it will act as a framework, helping to contain you within what would otherwise be a great expanse of wall."

COLORFUL SOLUTIONS

To transform a huge space into a comfortable one, select colors that are dark, saturated or warm. Kaufman claims that dark colors are the obvious solution, because they weight the space and envelop the inhabitants. Unfortunately, this often requires something of a leap of faith; many of us are terrified of dark colors, and therefore rarely select them. As Kaufman sees it, the fear usually stems from the difficulty in envisioning a paint manufacturer's color wheel on your wall. "People get the wrong impression of dark colors. They look at a tiny chip in front of their whitewashed walls, and panic." The trick, he says, is to always use much darker colors than normal. To get the desired color, his standard rule is two shades darker and two shades grayer, regardless of the size of the space. At the same time, he cautions against making any final selections without painting a mock-up or test strip. Many painters use large-scale mockups, often two feet by three feet in size, painted on poster or wallboard. These are certainly helpful, especially for decorative finishes, but for a big space, Kaufman recommends painting a 12 feet tall and 6 feet wide strip directly on the wall. "Paint your test strip, block off the rest of the room, remove the white drop cloths, and put furniture in front of it—because you will never see the color out of context. You will always think it's too dark."

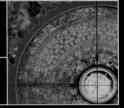

INSIDE
FENG SHUI

BY BENJAMIN HUNTINGTON

COLOR

Use bright colors to energize, and muted tones to calm down any space. The following colors represent the five elements of Feng Shui and can be used to enhance or reduce specific feelings in any area of the home.

- Using black or blue (the symbol of water) makes a space feel larger and quieter and will calm the space down.

- Using green (the symbol of wood) helps promote growth and understanding but can also, in limited amounts, provide an area of calm.

- Using red (the symbol of fire) will make a space feel smaller and stimulate activity.

- Using earth tones, yellows and browns (the symbol of earth), will create an area of grounding and inaction.

- Using white (the symbol of metal) creates an atmosphere of focus and thinking.

The intensity of the color is also important. If the color is bright, the feeling in the room will have more energy; if it's muted, the energy will be less apparent.

Saturated, bright colors will liven up a room. Interior designer Katie Ridder loves color and uses it whenever she can. "Color puts a smile on my face," says Ridder. "It warms up a room, gives it a personality." But she finds that it's hard to convince people to use color. Her recommendation for getting over the fear of using color is to start small. "Sometimes I introduce color in the form of accent pillows or art. This is often enough inspiration, and the clients agree to go for it."

"I'm not afraid of color," states Miles Redd, a hip, young designer who recently completed a very Hermés-orange-colored living room. Like many professionals, Redd chooses an object or feature, such as a fabric, artwork, or antique, to serve as the centerpiece of the room's palette. "I usually determine my color palette based upon the ground color, especially if there is a rug. For a recent project, we started with a lovely antique Turkish Oushak rug. It had a delicious orangey hue, and was a great jumping off point."

For a large Park Avenue apartment in New York, Noriega-Ortiz saturated the dining room with color. He chose warm colors: regal golds and luscious reds. "Gold-colored dining rooms are wonderful, because everyone looks good in gold, the skin just glows. And when people sit down to dinner they are framed by the walls behind them. Also, food looks scrumptious against gold; it looks fresh and cooked to perfection. Food looks terrible next to blue, it gets a gray cast—we learned that the hard way."

Kaufman points out that if the dining room is large enough, you can have a blue dining room without turning the people and the food an unpleasing shade of gray. He explains, "If the room is wide, but not too tall, you can paint the walls blue and the ceiling cream. In this scenario, the light will reflect off the ceiling and down onto the people sitting at the table."

TOP This dark blue would have seemed over-the-top had the designer not known what was going in front of it. Always choose colors on site, painting a large test strip and placing furniture or fabrics in front of it. Designed by Paul Silverman.

BOTTOM Many designers get color inspiration from an object. In this living room, the orangey wall color was selected from one of the rich hues in the antique Persian rug. Designed by Ned Marshall Inc.

"If you do not add depth and interest with color, the only other way is with a glaze or a decorative finish." — DONALD KAUFMAN

Famed interior and furniture designer Barbara Barry has a different take on which colors seem intimate and soothing. With her business based in gridlocked Los Angeles, she has a healthy respect for the color green. "I live in a world colored by a green lens. That doesn't mean I only work in green, but you cannot find a room I have done without it." Barry believes that the eye delights in the nuance of different values of the same hue, or different hues of the same value. "For instance, our senses are massaged and calmed when we look at the ocean with its infinite variations of blue-green. We become more tranquil in calm environments and are able to absorb more. In this fast-paced world, that is no small thing."

The Color Marketing Group, an international, not-for-profit association of more than 1,700 color and design professionals who forecast color trends, agrees with Barry. They project that today's consumers will want colors that provide a respite from technology and reflect a return to nature. Popular colors will be earth-based in tone: greens, mustards, ochres, umbers, etc.

According to Kaufman, the paint manufacturers also follow color trends: "They want you to change your colors all the time—you must have the latest color! But we don't subscribe to that theory. We think a good color is a good color."

But Kaufman's definition of a good color differs significantly from that of the paint companies. "All of the manufacturers are great with paint, and terrible with color," he explains. Every can of paint, regardless of the brand, is made up of the same components: pigment, binder and liquid. The difference lies in the blending. While most manufacturers use only two or three pigments to create each color, Kaufman adds dozens of pigments, representing a full color spectrum and resulting in a final

Golden dining rooms flatter the diners and make the food look more appetizing. Designed by Benjamin Noriega-Ortiz.

Paint finishes can affect the feel of an interior. The glossy finish used in this colorful library is inherently light and reflective. Designed by Ilemeau et cie.

Using paint to highlight certain details, such as chair rails or a specific part of the crown or base molding, helps to create a finished look. Designed by Llana Wyman.

Layers of color in this Venetian-red room result in a luminous,
multi-hued finish that contains all the colors of the spectrum.
Designed by Dennis Connel.

color that gives surfaces extra luminosity and depth. "In a large space, you need to have added interest," he says. "If you do not add that depth and interest with color, the only other way is with a glaze or a decorative finish."

DECORATIVE PAINT/PATTERN

"One flat color, especially in a big room, leads to one bland space," theorizes decorative painter Vesna Bricelj. Decorator Tracey Winn Pruzan of Cullman & Kravis concurs, maintaining that her firm hardly ever paints just one color on the wall, opting instead to utilize a layered finish. And in large spaces, especially the public rooms, they often opt for a darker shade as well. She states, "We don't just paint a living room peach. Instead we would prefer to do a washed-out, multi-hued Venetian red." Pruzan thinks that the problem with selecting a single color is that flat latex paints are essentially dead, having no light-reflecting properties. The benefit of applying layered or glazed finishes is that they look different at different times of the day, and this adds another dimension to the overall design of a room. Pruzan also points out that they often take the design one step further, applying a stencil design over the glazed finish. Pruzan and other designers at Cullman & Kravis work with companies such as SilverLining Interiors of New York City to realize these highly reflective surfaces that are visually stunning.

Though there have been numerous technological advances in materials, the actual techniques of decorative painting—such as marbleizing, leafing, gilding and glazing—haven't changed very much over the years. What makes the biggest impact is the hand of the artist. Agnus Liptak, founder of Fresco Decorative Painting, likes to compare decorative painting to cooking, where minute changes by an artist can produce a drastically different effect than that achieved by another artist using the same materials. Joshua Wiener, owner of SilverLining Interiors, reveals that Elissa Cullman of Cullman & Kravis usually requests that a different artist work in each room of a particular project, preferring to vary the touch of the artists' hands throughout the residence.

"Decorative paint is a great way to customize a space," states Thomas Jayne, who is known for his historically accurate interiors. Jayne does a lot of work with painted finishes, especially faux bois, due to the large quantities of wood paneling that were historically used in both American and European homes. He has found that faux bois is a wonderful way to overcome the expense and scarcity of the quality wood needed to restore or create

Decorative paint is a wonderful way to customize a space. With unlimited design possibilities, this powder room successfully mixes patterns and colors to achieve a unique look. Designed by Threadneedle Street of New Jersey.

Decorative artists can produce a wide variety of finishes, including faux metal, marble and verdigris. Designed by Vesna Bricelj.

"If the entire room is cream-colored, and you paint the ceiling the same hue, it could be uncomfortable. You paint it a gray-blue, which is very subtle, and the ceiling seems to come down." — DAVID EASTON

grandeur in today's large homes. Jayne also finds that artists working with faux marble and faux bois achieve better results when their work is slightly exaggerated. "This makes it more handsome," claims Jayne. "Photorealism in decorative painting is almost repulsive, and the use of it resulted in a predominance of bad decorative painting produced in the 1980s."

Vesna Bricelj takes Jayne's sentiment a step further. "I think it's more intimate to do a freehand version of an architectural detail, rather than attempt to fool the eye." In a New York City project, Bricelj painted her version of wrought iron; the artistic result is fun and whimsical. However, she also replicates architectural detail, for a fraction of the cost of architectural millwork. The most popular designs are faux paneling, faux molding, faux stone and faux mosaic.

Jayne has found that his clients will typically roll their eyes when he firsts suggests that they should implement a trompe l'oeil solution. Like designer Katie Ridder's approach to introducing color, Jayne often starts with a small detail, such as marbleized baseboards. In his experience, painting the bases a dark faux marble provides the visual weight necessary to hold down a large space.

Today's designers are not only painting the walls. In large spaces, the ceiling is very visible, and needs to be addressed. During his days working with Parish Hadley, Jayne adopted Albert Hadley's technique of painting living room ceilings a bold color that reflects down onto the rest of the room. However, instead of using Hadley's signature pink, Jayne prefers to use a greenish-gray shade of black that works to hold down high ceilings, creating a more intimate setting. David Easton also subscribes to this theory: "If the entire room is cream-colored, and you paint the ceiling the same hue, it could be very uncomfortable.

INSIDE
FENG SHUI
BY BENJAMIN HUNTINGTON

PATTERNS

Strong linear patterns tend to be more eye-catching and therefore create a more "Yang" or energetic feeling in a space.

Curved lines and random patterns tend to soften a space, creating a more "Yin" or calming feeling.

Patterns that replicate nature are an important part of Feng Shui. All people need the constant reminder of our connection to nature (the Tao), and using patterns and textures as symbols of nature is important in all of our surroundings. These images can be as simple as a natural wood finish or a printed leaf pattern on a fabric.

You paint it a gray-blue, which is very subtle, and the ceiling seems to come down. Suddenly the space works."

Incorporating motifs and colors from other aspects of the room, Katie Ridder stencils patterns on the ceiling, adds color to moldings, and generally uses paint to create a finished look. "Using paint and decoration on the ceiling is just an extra detail, it helps create a cohesive look," she says.

> "Wallpaper can be very effective in large spaces, but it's a tricky situation. If the scale is too small, it can make the entire room look ditsy." — MATTHEW PATRICK SMYTH

FINISHES

Finishes, like color, are dependent on the light and existing site conditions, so it's difficult to generalize about the results. However, there are a couple rules of thumb:

Typically, a bright, glossy finish is lighter and more reflective, which leads to a space that feels larger. Matte paint absorbs the light and keeps the walls opaque and less reflective, therefore more enclosed. Kaufman claims that flat paint always gives the greatest depth, regardless of the color.

PAINT FINISHES

Manufacturers offer a wide variety of finishes with many different names, but most fall into one of the three following categories:

MATTE OR FLAT
Matte paint produces a classic suede-like finish, especially appropriate for walls and ceilings. Matte dries to a non-reflective, dead-flat finish. It's particularly attractive when accented with brilliant or satin eggshell finishes on doors, window frames and trim. The elastic properties of matte paint help bridge any small cracks in the painted surface and help hide surface flaws. Matte paint is also suitable for rooms subject to humidity variations, such as the bathroom. It absorbs and then releases excess moisture, unlike glossy finishes.

SATIN EGGSHELL
Satin eggshell is a versatile finish that can be used on a variety of surfaces, such as wood, plaster, wallboard, metal and plastic. It's an appropriate finish for a number of applications, such as walls, ceilings, doors, trim, railings, baseboards, moldings, cabinets, furniture and window frames. Using this paint finish results in a lovely understated sheen that's the key to its versatility. It's an easily maintained and washable finish that can cover minor flaws. When applied over two coats of brilliant enamel in the same color, this finish can also be used for exterior projects including doors, trim and shutters.

BRILLIANT OR GLOSSY
Brilliant paint finish can be used on interior and exterior surfaces for an ultra-glossy sheen. Paints with a brilliant finish can be used on wood, plaster, wallboard, plastic and all metals. The durability of the brilliant finish makes it a good choice for covering doors, trim, railings, cabinets, wainscoting, furniture, exterior architectural façades, shutters and garden furniture. When applied to perfectly smooth walls and ceilings, brilliant paint provides maximum protection and depth of color with a mirror-like luminescence that can be used subtly or dramatically to create focus, space and light.

But there are always exceptions. Bricelj painted an oversized oval-shaped dining room in a nontraditional grayish-blue. Despite the cool color, the room felt luminous and warm. Bricelj explains that the result was due to the unusual finish, "It had a striking pearlescent glow that seemed to catch the light, creating a sense of warmth not usually felt with blues."

Pattern can also be achieved through juxtaposing various finishes. For example, decorative painter Chuck Hettinger loves creating innovative designs, such as his "invisible stencil," where he uses a stencil technique to paint a pattern in gloss finish over a flat background of the same color. The artist believes this type of finish is playful, yet elegant, and works best in interiors that can be viewed at an angle, such as hallways.

WALLCOVERING

In addition to the wide variety of painted finishes, there's a plethora of wallcovering options. Today's choices aren't limited to wallpaper, as they are as likely to be made of fabric, vinyl or natural fibers such as grasscloth, leather or even horsehair. Designers love the unlimited possibilities that wallcovering provides, including texture, depth, scenics, delineation of spaces, focal points, themes, tonal variety, color, etc. All of these can create successful solutions to daunting spaces.

WALLPAPER

Credit for traditional wallpaper, as we know it, must go to the Chinese. As early as 200 BC, they began hand-painting papers to hang as wall decorations. In the 700s, wallpaper became westernized, as the Arabs introduced paper making

to Europe. However, most medieval interiors were cold, damp and drafty, and wallpaper was replaced by heavier and more practical wall hangings such as tapestries and hides of leather. Painted papers would have to wait for their heyday until the 18th century, when the upper classes would master the use of decorative prints. The Victorians were so adept that they could layer up to seven different patterns in one room, dividing the walls into three distinct areas: dado, fill-

ing and frieze, with an additional decorating area on the ceiling. In fact, according to Bradbury & Bradbury, an art wallpaper manufacturer, one of the hallmarks of the Victorian era was the careful coordination of wall and ceiling patterns. The decoration included wonderfully imaginative combinations of borders, panels, corner fans and rosettes. (Certain prestigious companies continue to make wallpapers to historic specifications—see the appendix.)

Wallpaper on the entire expanse of a large room can be overwhelming. Consider papering only certain areas, such as the area above the wainscoting or other architectural detail. Designed by Katie Ridder and Peter Pennoyer.

BORDERS

The Victorians, with their wallpaper expertise, were on to something. According to Donald Kaufman, the border, whether it's a wallpaper motif or a painted molding, is a vital component to a large wallpapered space. Pattern, unless it's handled correctly, makes a space seem bigger, rather than the other way around. Think of tiny powder rooms or dormer bedrooms, where the paper continues up onto the ceiling—the room looks bigger because the borders between the wall and ceiling are dissolved. Kaufman explains, "Your eye naturally gravitates toward contrast; when there is none, the eye assumes the space continues." Therefore it's important to have lines of demarcation when using patterned wallpaper in a large space. Like the Victorians, think of breaking up the wall, using either architectural motifs—dado, chair rail, crown molding, etc.—or the equivalent in wallpaper or paint.

SCALE

Scale is another important component of wallcovering. Top interior designer Matthew Patrick Smyth cautions clients when they choose wallpaper with a pattern. "Wallpaper can be very effective in large spaces, but it's a tricky situation. If the scale is too small, it can make the entire room look ditsy." Pay attention when selecting all-over repeated pattern wallpaper—choose a motif that has weight to it.

SCENICS

If picking a suitable scale for an all-over repeated pattern seems too complicated, there are other options, such as scenic or mural-style papers.

Well-known for its gorgeous Chinese-inspired

TOP Gracie Studio makes wallpapers the way it was done in the 18th century—each one is hand-painted with great attention to detail. BOTTOM Wallpaper is an excellent way to decorate a wall. This wallpaper not only incorporates architectural-type details such as crown molding, applied paneling and chair rail, but also offers an assortment of artwork. Designed by Noel Jeffrey.

This large dining room hosts a figurative, mural-style paper. Though the walls of the room have a blue cast, the ceiling is painted white, which softly reflects light down onto the diners and the surface of the table. Designed by Benjamin Noriega-Ortiz.

In addition to wallpaper and paint, there are many other materials that can embellish walls, such as this rich red leather punctuated with brass studs. The dark color is enveloping, while the grid of metal adds definition to the wall's expanse. Designed by Peter Pennoyer and Katie Ridder.

prints, Gracie Studio, maker of custom, hand-painted wall-papers, has papered many large houses and apartments around the world. Mike Gracie, vice president of Gracie Studio, says approximately 80 percent of their papers are used in residential dining rooms, with bedrooms and stair-wells as popular second choices. He believes that the figurative, mural-style papers work best in large spaces, because there's room to stand back and admire the entire scene, rather than focus only on a small section. The typical Gracie paper is made in panels that are 3 feet wide and 10 feet tall, a size that is based on papers made in China during the 1700s and 1800s for export. With the his-toric muted color-palette, the papers have a wonderful soft glow. (Custom colors and sizes are available.)

OTHER OPTIONS

Taking cues from history, designers can line walls with fabric or leather to add interest and a sense of warmth to a space. In a large library in a Park Avenue apartment, Miles Redd, while working with Bunny Williams, decided to cover the walls with leather decorated with nail heads. "We went back and forth about this room. We considered doing mahogany paneling, which the client loved, but she likened that look to a classic navy blue blazer. She wanted elements of it, only updated." The result was a nod to French designer Jean Michel Frank, who typically covered walls in parchment-colored leathers—whereas Redd's library was sheathed in gorgeous, deep green leather. "The client was a bit nervous that the color might be too dark, so we framed it with medium tone, iced-tea colored wood moldings—which breaks it up. And I thought the room was very successful," states Redd.

PUNCH LIST

☐ Paint and wallcovering are flexible, cost-effective and fast solutions, adding definition to large spaces.

☐ Light and locale are instrumental factors when choosing colors.

☐ Dark, saturated and warm colors enclose a space and make it more intimate.

☐ Paint large test strips in the space before choosing colors. Observe at all times of the day.

☐ Decorative paint is a great way to customize a space.

☐ Don't forget to decorate the ceiling—many designers paint tall ceilings in darker colors to add visual weight.

☐ Paint comes in a variety of finishes—choose one based on your location and requirements.

☐ Horizontal breaks (painted moldings, border papers) create lines of demarcation, and help stop the optical effects of pattern.

☐ Be careful of the scale of pattern on wallpaper: use large-scale patterns or scenics for big spaces.

☐ Do not continue wallpaper onto the ceiling in a tall room; it will only make it look taller.

A successfully decorated room combines a workable seating arrangement around a suitable focal point, with symmetrical elements (such as the bookcases on either side of the fireplace) and the right mix of fabrics and colors. Designed by Katie Ridder and Peter Pennoyer.

CHAPTER 6

DECORATING DETAILS
FURNITURE & FABRIC

A successful interior design is like a recipe—the outcome depends upon the quality of the ingredients, and the order in which they're combined. It involves coordinating specific styles and types of furniture, upholstering them in the

appropriate fabrics, with suitable colors and patterns, and arranging the ensemble in just the right fashion. A designer may start the process with an idea or inspiration, but it all comes together with the furniture floor plan.

MAPPING OUT THE PLAN

The floor plan is a two-dimensional, top-down view of a room, complete with all architectural features. Before they go shopping for furniture or fabrics, interior designers use these outlines as starting points to determine what's necessary. The scale and layout of the room, together with the needs of the homeowner, will dictate the type of furniture required and the number, size and style of the items, as well as the optimal configuration.

In the initial stages of design, floor plans help to visualize the relationships between the furniture and space. Benjamin Noriega-Ortiz believes furnishing a room starts with geometry: "The size and shape of a room dictates what type of furniture you will use—your furniture must relate to the space." Following this principle, Noriega-Ortiz specified a round table, custom-made by Wood & Hogan, for a large, square dining room in a classically designed apartment in New York. "If you have a square room, you need to use a round, square or octagonal table. If you put a rectangular table in a square room, you will have an area of the room that is smaller than the other—it's not symmetrical."

The placement of this dressing table in the window was a direct result of the layout of the room and the homeowner's needs. Designed by Cullman & Kravis.

IT'S ALL IN THE SYMMETRY

Symmetry and balance lead to a comfortable interior. Every interior is composed of a series of lines: horizontal, vertical and curved, made up by the edges of the furnishings and architecture—the walls, windows, moldings and doors. The eye tends to find comfort in things that are aligned and centered. If the architecture of a room is off balance, it needs to be compensated for by some other design element. Katie Ridder embraces the theory. "For me, symmetry is really important. I'm known for my quirkiness, and I love that of course, but it doesn't work without symmetry." With this concept in mind, she often coordinates the key items of the décor, such as the built-ins, bookcases or large furniture pieces, to the lines of the architecture. For example, in the very large, formal living room of a San Francisco townhouse, Ridder inherited an existing scenario of one small bookcase next to a very small fireplace. She explains, "The fireplace wall was a main focal point for the room. It was directly opposite the entrance, and the proportions of the bookcase and mantel were so off-kilter to the architecture. So we removed the small bookcase, and built two large matching ones flanking the fireplace." In addition, Ridder reconfigured the mantel, hunting through the flea markets of Paris to find an antique fireplace surround complete with *trumeaux*, a columned area for a mirror, that added height and a sense of grandeur. The result was a wall filled with decorative items well suited to the scale of the architecture.

DAVID EASTON'S FURNITURE CHECKLIST

(In Order of Importance)

1. Mantel (or other large focal point)

2. Upholstered pieces (sofas, armchairs, chaises, ottomans)

3. Rug or other floor treatment

4. Ceiling light fixture (chandelier, lantern, etc.)

5. Additional furnishings (side tables, coffee tables, cabinets, occasional chairs)

This round dining table relates well to the square-shaped dining room; furniture placement begins with basic geometric relationships. Designed by Benjamin Noriega-Ortiz.

POINT OF FOCUS: MANTELS

All successful interiors need a focal point, or an anchor, around which the furniture layout is situated. As in Ridder's living room, fireplaces are a popular choice, both historically and today. Fire plays both a functional and a symbolic role. In addition to providing warmth, light and a means to cook food, it offers a sense of physical comfort and well-being. "The fireplace is a hugely important element on so many levels," confirms acclaimed Washington, D.C.-based designer Mary Douglas Drysdale. "People want to gather around it, even when it is not lit."

David Easton believes the mantel is an indispensable part of his furnishings plan: "To me a mantel is a piece of furniture—the most important piece." If a room has a fireplace opening, Easton always chooses the mantel before selecting any other furnishings. He believes it's a natural focal point, and dictates the size, scale and style of all other items in the room. "It is the first step in determining the spatial relationship between the architecture and the interiors."

TOP Relating decorative elements to the architecture of a room creates a sense of harmony. In this interior the bookcase height matches up with the dropped soffit. Designed by Beverley Ellsley. BOTTOM A mantel is a natural and historical focal point to anchor the seating arrangement in a room. Designed by Nancy Mannucci.

PREVIOUS PAGE Symmetry is created by flanking a new mantel with matching floor lamps and built-in bookcases. Designed by Katie Ridder and Peter Pennoyer. ABOVE Many designers find it easiest to work from the ground up. Here, the red floral rug served as a starting point, inspiring the style and color for the rest of the interior. Designed by Llana Wyman.

If you want to make the fireplace the focal point of the room, but the existing mantel is not ideal, and changing it is not an option, there are other decorating techniques used by the pros to add emphasis. To visually add height, Benjamin Noriega-Ortiz often hangs an impressive mirror or places a grand floral arrangement above the mantel. (See Chapter 7, *The Right Stuff*, for more information.) For a different approach, try Katie Ridder's method of painting the fireplace surround in a contrasting, eye-catching color, such as vivid orange in a pale lilac room. These tricks call attention to the area, indicating that the fireplace is a significant feature of the room.

(Regardless of design, when adding, constructing or altering a fireplace, it's imperative to contact a professional, preferably an architect or fireplace specialist. To ensure safety, it's vital to comply with all regulations and building codes for fireplace construction. If you're considering a change to any fireplace treatment, expert advice is not only useful, it's essential.)

POINT OF FOCUS: OTHER OPTIONS

Different designers have different ideas about what makes the best starting point when determining a furniture layout. Many choose to work from the ground up, starting with the area rug. This can be an excellent tool for framing a certain area and accentuating how a room is used. (See Chapter 3, *Crafting the Plan*, for further explanation.) David Easton typically divides ungainly large spaces into a series of odd-numbered configurations, such as one, three, or five—a system championed by the Greeks. If he doesn't articulate these areas with architectural treatments, he often uses area rugs. For example, if he decides to subdivide a space into three areas, Easton will usually

INSIDE
FENG SHUI

BY BENJAMIN HUNTINGTON

FURNITURE PLACEMENT

■ Always make sure that the furniture you use is in good repair and is stable.

■ Never place a piece of furniture so that it impedes the full opening of any door.

■ Try not to place light furniture (i.e. with tall, thin legs) on a stair landing.

■ Avoid placing a tall bookcase or oversized piece of furniture so that it can be seen at the head of a staircase as you ascend.

ENTRY AREA

■ The furniture on the right as you enter is the most important.

■ Make sure that the furniture in this area is not oversized and does not make the entry area feel crowded.

■ An area carpet in this space is almost always a great benefit.

CONTINUED ON PAGE 130

In a large room, it is important to create several seating areas that will comfortably accommodate both small and large gatherings. Designed by Katie Ridder and Peter Pennoyer.

TOP Rugs work well for defining an area or subdividing a room without any architectural changes. Designed by Samuel Botero. BOTTOM If there is no mantel in a room, you can create a focal point using a substantial piece of furniture, and adding significance with artwork. Designed by Brian J. McCarthy.

These chairs are large in scale, but the lightness of the arms and legs acts as a counterfoil to keep them from appearing over-sized. Designed by Benjamin Noriega-Ortiz.

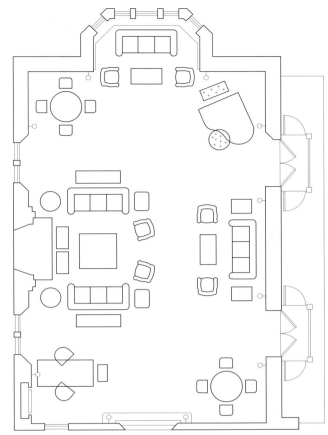

create one large group in the middle of the room on a large rug, bordered by two smaller arrangements on smaller rugs. The rugs, rather than the walls, act as the dividers between the seating areas. He explains, "Rugs are critical because they define the planned area."

Decorator Miles Redd also works from the floor up, because, he says, it can be very difficult to find the perfect rug—especially if the desired rug is an antique that needs to fit within the existing parameters of a space. "If you find the rug first, it is much easier to go out and find the appropriate fabrics and furnishings. I start with a beautiful rug, and build up."

PLOTTING THE SEATING CHART

Once you've settled on a focal point, it's time to figure out the furniture layout. Like David Easton, most designers decorating a large room will arrange furniture into multiple seating areas, with the main grouping centered around the focal point. Matthew Patrick Smyth cautions homeowners against creating just one seating area in a big room. He says, "One large seating area with more than eight or ten people would be very noisy, and not everyone would be able to participate in the conversation." Smyth recommends that seating areas not exceed six or eight people, with the ideal configuration being one major seating area with complementary minor areas. "The main seating group should accommodate approximately eight people, with your secondary seating groups holding four to six." He says people naturally break up into smaller conversational groups, and the room should be able to accommodate this, especially if it's going to be used for entertaining.

Whether the room will accommodate one person or twenty, designer Elissa Cullman says there are

TOP This floor plan illustrates how a large room can be successfully broken down into several seating areas using effective furniture placement. Note the seven separate seating areas. Designed by Cullman & Kravis.

BOTTOM Repeating shapes and patterns within an interior leads to harmony and balance. In this dining room, the designer reprised the grid pattern of the parquet floor in the checks on the curtains, while repeating the circles and squares of the ceiling in the shapes of the dining room chairs. Designed by Noel Jeffrey.

INSIDE
FENG SHUI

LIVING ROOM (MAIN GATHERING SPACE)

- Try to arrange the seating so that most people, when seated, can see the entry to this area, or at least see it in a mirror.

- Do not place tall or oversized pieces of furniture directly behind seating groups.

- If the back of a sofa is seen from the entry door, put a sofa table there with a solid object on it (a statue or a large pair of lamps).

- If there are many large windows in the space, use furniture that looks heavy and sits directly on the floor, rather than furniture that has tall, thin legs.

BEDROOMS

- Keep large pieces of furniture away from the bed.

- Try not to position the head of the bed against a window. If you have no choice, then use very heavy curtains.

- Try not to position the bed with the foot facing the entry door. If you have no choice, then use a bed with a footboard.

- Avoid having one side of a bed pushed up against a wall, and try to always have bedside tables, with their own lamps or lights, on each side of the bed.

- Make sure there is some airspace, even a small amount, under the bed.

several important rules to follow: "From every seat in the room a person should be able to talk to someone if they want to, see the print on any sort of reading material, and put a drink down on either a coffee table or side table. No single piece of furniture should be off on its own—that's too isolating."

David Easton likens this process of plotting out furnishing arrangements to the composition of music. "As in music, interior design is full of rhythm, harmony and balance. I think of furniture as the counterpoint (to use a musical term) to the architecture." When placing furniture onto the floor plan, Easton takes great care to achieve balance. He explains, "The spaces between items have a certain shape and weight; they must be balanced by the weight of the furnishings." Easton also repeats certain shapes and details throughout the space, such as reprising the arc of a round table in the slope of a curved sofa. "If you get your repeated elements just right, the space is music; if you don't, then the space is dead."

PICKING UP THE PIECES

Today's furniture market is vast, filled with thousands of options, from antiques and reproductions to custom upholstery and modern renditions. To give the project direction, and narrow down the huge array of choices, designers again take cues from the architecture and the required function of the space. With a very large room, it's important that the furniture have a certain presence or visual weight. With the abundance of options available, it's possible to play with the scale of the furniture, making it deeper, taller or more massive, but experts say there's a fine line between what's comfortable to the human figure and what isn't. Smyth agrees that large

Fabric is incredibly versatile—it helps to soften an interior in a variety of ways, ornamenting anything from a wall, doorway or window to a table or bed. Designed by Joanne DePalma.

130 BIG HOME, BIG CHALLENGE

spaces allow for large-scale furniture, but he says, "Over-size does not mean out-of-scale. I've seen interiors with gigantic furniture, and the whole place looks like *Alice in Wonderland*."

Most designers agree that furniture should be comfortable as well as stylish. Ridder is unyielding when it comes to comfort. She routinely specifies all custom upholstery so that she has the ability to play with the scale and style, yet maintain a suitable level of comfort.

"The upholstered pieces are so important in a room—they are like sculpture. It is imperative that they be right," says Easton. Custom upholstery is an important fac-

tor in interior design, according to the professionals, but it's often confusing and elusive for homeowners. "The ability to understand upholstery is a cultural problem, and society as a whole must first learn to appreciate it," explains Bruno Lopez, owner of La Chaise de France in Easthampton, Massachusetts. "If you live in Europe you see upholstery everywhere, and a higher value is placed on it. In America, high-end upholstery has become a ghost trade." Lopez suggests that there's a big difference between the quality, look and feel of upholstery built using traditional techniques and the assembly-line pieces that are turned out by large manufacturers today. He espouses the benefits of traditional upholstery done by hand in the way it was done in the 18th century. Albert Fisher, co-owner of Versailles Drapery & Upholstery, believes that quality is very important, but says it doesn't matter what method is used to achieve it. "The most important thing is how a client feels when they sit in a chair," he says. In the end, scale and comfort are paramount.

To create a cohesive look in an interior, the experts advise keeping the scale and style of all the furniture consistent. When describing the characteristics of a piece of furniture, a designer will typically refer to the "limbs," or rather the arms and legs of the piece. The details are traditionally rendered in the limbs, whether it is style or scale. For example, look at the straight, narrow leg of a neoclassical chair, versus the robust, curved leg and cross stretchers of a Renaissance one. Try to select and harmonize items that have a similar mass and height. And remember that it's important to have a mix of furniture with legs and furniture with skirts. Elissa Cullman explains that a room with too many legs can seem busy and out of date. "It's too much like a period room—it just doesn't look current or modern."

Upholstery pieces are important elements in a room, creating a statement with their size, style and color. In this interior, the screen behind the sofa acts as a framework that accentuates the seating area. Designed by Noel Jeffrey.

SMALL-SCALE SUCCESS

Though it's best to use large-scale furnishings in grand spaces, it's also possible to use small pieces effectively. In a huge Palm Beach residence, Benjamin Noriega-Ortiz was faced with the challenge of incorporating his client's collection of dainty antique furniture. "This project is an example of a woman who loves tiny things, yet lives in a large house," he explains. In a living room with 20-foot ceilings, Noriega-Ortiz had to come up with a way to make the client's delicate settees, petite piecrust tables and tiny footstools not get lost. "All of her furniture looked so tiny and low in this double-height room, so I hung a huge curtain of lightweight fabric from the ceiling, and tied it back with a cord at the exact height of the furniture. The graceful curve of the drape brings the eye down, inviting you to sit." To draw additional attention to the seating area, Noriega-Ortiz added a few key pieces of furniture, such as a substantial George Smith sofa and ottoman. "The sofa is inviting—its back is higher, so it creates a sort of alcove."

In a double-height room filled with low antique furniture, this unconventional solution works well—a giant curtain tied back with a cord brings the eye down to the height of the seating. Designed by Benjamin Noriega-Ortiz.

FABRIC GLOSSARY

Appliqué: A technique of applying (usually by embroidery) pieces of fabric to a ground to create a design.

Batik: A traditional Indonesian textile, printed with dye and wax.

Block-Print: A fabric created by one of the oldest methods of printing, which uses carved wooden blocks with a pattern cut in relief.

Botanical: A design showing a plant form or forms, rendered as in a botanical illustration.

Bouclé: A fabric with a looped surface, suitable for upholstery.

Broadcloth: Originally from England, a double-width, woolen, plain-woven fabric.

Brocade: A complicated woven fabric with a rich surface pattern and matte background. Originally woven from silk, today made from all fibers.

Buckram: A heavy linen or cotton fabric, often used for backing softer, lighter fabrics.

Burlap: A coarse cloth made of jute fiber. Used originally for sacking. Today firm, narrow widths are used as tapes and trims.

Calico: Any inexpensive printed cotton. Originally a plain white or printed cotton fabric imported from Calicut, India.

Cambric: A firm, fine, plain-woven cotton or linen fabric, which is often finished with a slight sheen. Predominantly used for linens on pillows and duvets.

Canvas: A strong, heavy linen or cotton fabric woven to make it waterproof.

Challis: A soft woolen fabric printed with a small floral design.

Chenille: A woven fabric made from a tufted weft yarn, which creates a fuzzy pile.

Chinoiserie: Any western interpretation of an oriental design.

Chintz: A glazed cotton fabric, often with large-scale floral designs.

Contemporary: A fabric design featuring simple, extremely stylized, often bold motifs.

Corduroy: A sturdy, medium or heavyweight cotton or synthetic pile fabric with evenly spaced, regular ridges running down the length of cloth.

Crewelwork: Elaborate, textural stitching that creates a surface pattern on a thick, woven-cotton ground cloth.

Damask: A reversible satin fabric in which the figures or patterns are defined by the contrast of the shiny warp and the matte weft.

Duck: A firmly woven fabric, usually cotton, similar to canvas in appearance.

Flannel: A smooth fabric made from pressed wool, traditionally used for men's hats and suits; it's also appropriate for upholstery.

Gauze: Soft, sheer, woven fabric.

Gingham: A yarn-dyed, cotton or polyester fabric woven with checks, stripes or plaids, usually of white and one other color.

Ikat: Tribal-looking fabric woven with resist-dyed warp and weft.

Jacquard: Intricately patterned fabric made from a mechanical loom invented by Joseph Marie Jacquard in 1800.

Kilim: A cotton or wool fabric like tapestry, characterized by narrow divisions between the areas of pattern.

Lace: A delicate, openwork fabric made by intricately twisting and knotting cotton thread.

Linen: A strong cloth woven from flax.

Madras: A brightly colored cotton fabric woven into checked or square designs—originally from the Indian city of Madras.

Moiré: A ribbed fabric (usually silk or acetate) with a wavy, watered appearance woven into the fabric or produced by heat and pressure.

Muslin: A plain, woven cotton fabric, which varies in texture from fine to coarse, and is either very tightly or loosely woven (like cheesecloth).

Organdy: Made from a very fine cotton yarn with a slightly stiff and starchy finish.

Paisley: A fabric with stylized curving floral or fruit forms, derived from patterns originating in India. The pattern can be printed or woven.

Plush: Generic term for a soft, thick fabric with evenly cut pile, similar to velvet, but with a less dense, longer pile.

Poplin: A cotton fabric with horizontal ribs, formed by using weft threads that are thicker than the warp threads.

Provençal: Country-French textile designs derived from 18th-century wood block prints, usually comprised of small-scale patterns.

Satin: A plain, warp-faced woven fabric with a smooth, lustrous surface and dull back.

Shantung: Originally from China, a soft, unfinished silk fabric.

Silk: One of the most luxurious of all furnishing fabrics, silk is made from the delicate threads of silkworm cocoons.

Striae: A stripe that changes subtly in color and/or texture from the top to the bottom of the fabric.

Tabby: A type of weave in which warp and weft cross each other at right angles. This technique is used for a wide range of fabrics, including taffeta, muslin and canvas.

Taffeta: A crisp, plain-woven fabric, with subtle surface ribs. Traditionally made from silk.

Tapestry: Heavy, woven fabric often depicting pictorial scenes.

Ticking: A strong, striped linen or cotton twill that is typically used for mattresses and bedding.

Toile de Jouy: A printed cotton fabric originally manufactured in the French town of Jouy-en-Josas. Usually depicts a fine-line, one-color scenic print.

Tweed: A plain or twill woven, woolen fabric originally from Scotland.

Twill: A basic weave with a diagonal grain, obtained by floating the weft over and under several warps.

Velvet: A thick, luxurious cut-pile fabric, which is formed by lifting the warp threads over wires and then cutting them.

Warp: The threads that run lengthwise in a woven fabric, crossed at right angles to the weft.

Weft: The horizontal threads interlaced through the warp in a woven fabric.

Worsted: A smooth fabric made using carded and combed wool yarn from a special breed of sheep.

Another fabulous find of Noriega-Ortiz's was an antique twist on the traditional wing chair. "The sides continue up over your head, so you feel protected—it works perfectly in such a tall space," he says.

WARP + WEFT = FABRIC

Interior designers today know that nothing sets the mood of an interior more clearly than fabrics; the texture, the pattern, the hand, the thickness and the weave all contribute to the overall style. The character of any room, whether it's formal and historically based or fresh and whimsical, can be deduced easily from the design of the fabric. Therefore, it's essential, particularly in a large space, that the selection be suited to the size, style and scale of both the furnishings and the architecture.

ENDLESS VARIETY

Though the construction of fabric is fairly consistent—there are three basic weaving systems: the tabby, the twill and the satin—the variations are unlimited. According to Janice Langrall, marketing director of F. Schumacher, there are thousands and thousands of fabrics on the market, and it's helpful to have an idea of what you're looking for before you shop.

Designers tend to focus their fabric search on key details, such as whether they want a woven or a print, an upholstery- or a curtain-weight, a solid or a pattern. Experts generalize that certain fabrics connote certain qualities. For example, fabrics with rough natural fibers and vivid geometrical patterns are inherently more masculine and modern, as opposed to pictorial prints on smooth cottons and silks, which seem more classical and feminine.

Locality also comes into play, as certain fabrics are more appropriate for particular locales than others. For example, velvet, mohair and thick wool would be warm and inviting in a cold climate, while crisp, cool cottons would be better suited to a warm climate. Seasonal shifts are also important to consider. What would be cozy in winter might appear sweltering in summer. For this reason, interior designers tend to pick intermediate fabrics, such as

In a master bedroom suite with a green scheme, the designer varied the print of the fabric and the intensity of the green to designate which areas of the suite were "his" and which were "hers." Designed by Cullman & Kravis.

The scale of the motif on this sofa's fabric helps make an
appropriate statement in the large, double-height living room.
Designed by Benjamin Noriega-Ortiz.

linen, heavy cotton or lightweight wool, for year-round upholstery, and seasonal fabrics for the details, including coverlets, throws and accent pillows. These smaller accessories can be changed easily and less expensively to create an atmosphere consistent with the season.

FABRIC NOTIONS

Fabric can be used in a wide variety of ways in an interior. Large amounts are needed for upholstery, curtain treatments and draped tables, while small pieces are useful for accents such as seat cushions and throw pillows. As with the furniture layout, it's important to balance the use of fabric by repeating certain motifs, colors and patterns throughout the room, taking care not to become either heavy-handed or monotonous.

Designer Elissa Cullman frequently utilizes a unifying theme to create a cohesive look and feel. For example, in a historic home on Long Island's north shore she specified a blue and white color scheme for one of the guest bedrooms. In addition to painting the room in the selected colors, Cullman chose a blue and white palette for the rug, bed skirt, upholstery pieces and curtain treatments. She varied the theme with the scale and motif of the patterns, using a check on the sofa, and a geometric grid softened by floral rosettes on the rug. Her design repeated an Asian-inspired print on the bed skirt, window treatment, supplementary seating, and some of the accent pillows. She explains, "Using the same fabric on the bed, upholstery and curtains makes you feel enveloped, almost like you're being embraced. It's a bedroom; you want it to feel intimate."

In the 50-foot-long living room of the same residence, in an unconventional act, Cullman decided to use a

TOP While the major elements—the curtains and upholstery—in this master suite were made of green fabrics, touches of blue were added in small details such as the throw on the chair. BOTTOM The repetition of the color blue throughout this bedroom creates a cohesive look and feel. Both projects designed by Cullman & Kravis.

plaid taffeta for the curtains. "This house is practically a castle. Built in 1928, its interiors are characterized by the late-Georgian detailing on a generous scale—with the main rooms decked out in baronial paneling. We wanted to tone down the formal aspect of the house. The plaid says, 'We're welcoming; we're homey.'"

Other designers also use curtain treatments to make a decorative statement, and sometimes as a solution to an out-of-scale problem. In a dining room on Park Avenue, Noriega-Ortiz used red window shades to draw attention away from the fact that the windows were out of scale. "Red is a very powerful color, it's an attention grabber," says the designer. "The windows were too tall; they just went on forever. And we wanted to keep the people's attention at a low level, around the dining table. So rather than doing a curtain in the same color as the walls, which

These dramatic red roller shades essentially cut the windows in half, leaving the exposed glass at the level of the dining table. Designed by Benjamin Noriega-Ortiz.

would have led the eye up, I visually cut the window in half with fixed, half-height, bright red Roman shades."

Curtain treatments run the risk of being overwhelming, particularly in a room filled with huge windows. Many designers caution against overly frilly and pronounced curtain designs. Katie Ridder says, "I don't like all the bells and whistles—the jabots and swags. I try to keep my designs fairly simple—just use a beautiful fabric and add beautiful detail, such as expert construction, high-quality hardware, and maybe a decorative motif, such as embroidery or a complementary fabric on the leading edge or valence."

Decorator Miles Redd says that he loves a grand window treatment, but not if it doesn't relate to the window. "There is nothing worse than a swag and jabot curtain on an eight-foot window. It just looks like a marshmallow sandwich." In most interiors, Redd says, he prefers a simple

Keeping curtain treatments simple is recommended in a space with lots of large windows. Add interest with complementary fabric as a trim. Designed by Mary Douglas Drysdale.

This elaborately draped table adds a sense of softness and flow to an otherwise hard space. Designed by Benjamin Noriega-Ortiz.

window treatment, "But, if you have the right scale interior and the right proportioned window, I say go for it."

FABRIC'S OTHER INCARNATIONS

In large spaces, carpet traditionally is the main way to soften and warm a room, but on occasion, the situation or design doesn't allow for one. In this scenario, designers often use fabric in creative and inventive ways to fill the void.

In the living room of a grand New York apartment, Noriega-Ortiz's clients did not want a rug. The clients had children, and they wanted them to be able to ride their bikes and run around in the large space. Noriega-Ortiz was faced with the challenge of designing something that would add softness to the space, yet still be functional. He came up with an elaborately draped table, engineered with wires that could lift up the excess fabric when the children were running around, but lower it for entertaining, giving a sumptuous look with volumes of fabric. "I was inspired by a couture skirt of Ralph Lauren's. It was ultra-full, with lots of creases and folds. This skirted table was a unique invention that works well in this space. If we didn't have this in the center of the room, it would be a very cold, hard room."

In Miles Redd's drawing room he chose not to put a rug, opting instead for dark chocolate parquet floors inlaid with polished silver. "I love the look of a crisp wood floor." To counteract all the crisp coolness, Redd upholstered the walls in a luscious pink silk. "Upholstered walls are a great way to add a sense of coziness to the room. And what a wonderful counterpoint to a tailored floor."

PUNCH LIST

☐ Decorating is the careful combination of furniture, fabrics, area rugs and other accent items.

☐ The first step to arranging furniture is to create a floor plan.

☐ When placing the furniture in the plan, symmetry, harmony, balance and scale all play important roles.

☐ Make sure to pick a focal point—perhaps a mantel, or a large item such as an antique armoire—to anchor the seating arrangement.

☐ In a large room, create several seating areas, limiting the maximum grouping to eight people.

☐ Rugs can be used as subdivisions in a room, acting as frameworks for specific seating areas.

☐ Take care that the weight and scale of the furnishings are balanced and compatible with the architecture.

☐ Repeat certain motifs, shapes and/or colors to give the room a cohesive look.

☐ Upholstery should be comfortable, and in scale with the human figure.

☐ The texture, pattern, hand, thickness and weave of fabrics all contribute to the overall character of a room.

☐ Relate the style of the fabric to both the style of the furniture and the architecture.

☐ Have an idea of what type of fabric you are looking for before you shop.

☐ Curtains and other window treatments are wonderful decorating opportunities, but take care that they don't become overwhelming.

In this New York townhouse, it is the art in the space that adds
a touch of warmth and personality to a very large living room.
Designed by Sidnam Petrone Gartner.

CHAPTER 7

THE RIGHT STUFF
ART & ACCESSORIES

With a large house come great rooms and big walls, which means many opportunities (and a big responsibility) to fill the space with personal effects. The job of filling it is made easier by the fact that everyone is a collector, in one form or another.

Collections of paintings, sculptures or accessories add atmosphere to the overall canvas of an interior. Designer Miles Redd says that art and accessories are vital to a room. "The two things that make an interior are books and artwork. If you don't have great things on the wall, then forget it." Decorative and fine art objects placed in a room contribute to the character and color scheme, as well as give insight into the personality of the owner. Whether it's a Picasso or a pinwheel, artwork and accessories help transform a large, impersonal house into a cozy, unique home.

Collections quickly set the tone and style of a space. Whereas one collector may choose a sedate gallery of works on paper, another may prefer the bold splash of contemporary paintings. A rustic grouping of African figurines exudes an exotic charm, while a glittering display of antique crystal decanters reflects a more refined ambience. Such objects, alone or grouped invitingly, can dramatically set the stage for the way a room is perceived. David Easton sums it up with a comparison: "There's a certain quality about a room that has a gray lacquer table with one square Japanese bowl on it, versus a traditional coffee table with a pair of candlesticks, a vase with flowers, books and other collectibles on it. Each gives a different attitude."

Collecting is a complicated and personal experience, but there are some guidelines and recommendations for how to utilize both fine art and art alternatives,

TOP Remember that everything on the wall, even books, adds character to a space. Designed by Joanne DePalma.
BOTTOM Collections come in all shapes and sizes—this glassware collection seems fitting gathered on top of a bureau. Designed by Nancy Mannucci.

such as mirrors and flowers, effectively in large spaces. The steps range from identifying, evaluating and purchasing art to hanging, displaying and coordinating it with the décor, as well as tips from experts on how to protect your investment.

PURCHASING ART

Most homeowners and many interior designers are wary about purchasing fine art, as it is a highly specialized field, requiring years of advanced study to gain expertise. New York-based designer Kitty Hawks says that although art and design have always had an intricate relationship, she's reluctant to get involved in art specification. "A designer must strike a careful balance between the art, architecture and décor, keeping in mind the personality and lifestyle of the client," she says. However, there are ways to overcome this anxiety, specifically by asking pertinent questions, and developing trusted relationships with experts, such as art advisors, galleries, dealers and/or auction houses.

According to a number of designers, it's imperative that, with or without the help of an interior designer, you develop a plan for outfitting the house with art. There are four central questions to answer before a project starts:

■ Do you have an art collection that you're passionate about?
■ If not, do you want to start a collection?
■ If neither is the case, do you merely want something attractive that will go with your home's interior?
■ If you aren't interested in fine art, would you consider art alternatives? (See "Art Alternatives" on page 148 for suggestions.)

If you have trouble answering the above questions, you may want to seek advice from an art expert.

When purchasing and hanging fine art, it often helps to have an expert's advice. These contemporary paintings are shown to their best advantage hung together in a series, turning the long hall into a gallery space. Designed by Sidnam Petrone Gartner.

TOP Art advisors can shop for anything, including architectural prints from specific historic buildings. Designed by Benjamin Noriega-Ortiz. BOTTOM If you do not have a collection of fine art, it is possible to come up with decorative alternatives, such as these vintage magazine covers. Designed by Mark Ziff.

Art advisors can help develop a plan, and assist in the task of finding the art that was envisioned.

Art advisors specialize in developing collections, traveling exhaustively in search of just the right object. Judith Selkowitz of Art Advisory Services has worked with hundreds of corporate and private clients, and has bought everything from a 102-foot mobile to a $200 antique English poster. The role of an art advisor in Selkowitz's mind is to take the guesswork out of buying art. "What I offer is the knowledge of a diverse selection of original art, as well as an inventory of slides from hundreds of artists. Additionally, I have an extensive group of contacts with museum directors, curators, gallery dealers, private collectors and artists located worldwide." Selkowitz also travels frequently to maintain firsthand knowledge of the current art market, scouting out emerging artists and trends so that she can quickly locate works of art that will appeal to her clients' tastes and criteria.

Many designers rely on art experts to find an appropriate piece for their designs. "The right painting makes the whole room," says Katie Ridder. "Furniture tends to be all one height, approximately 34 inches, which means in a large room with high ceilings, you're left with this massive expanse of blank wall that just seems to go up forever." In one of her projects, a San Francisco townhouse, Ridder sought just the right painting to fill that expanse. She turned to Tom Armstrong, a former director of New York City's Whitney Museum, for advice. With the client's input, Armstrong and Ridder selected all the art for the residence, including a mammoth contemporary painting by artist Albert Brooks for the 20-foot-tall living room. "Tom has a wonderful eye, and was instrumental in striking a successful balance in the interiors," says Ridder.

"Paintings and artwork give quality, accessories give personality, and mirrors give depth." — DAVID EASTON

LARGE-SCALE OBJECTS AND SELECT GROUPINGS

In large-scale spaces, it's important to use either large-scale objects or a select grouping of smaller items. Miles Redd says, "In a big room, I love a big, bold statement. But I have learned that a group of small paintings, hung correctly, can make just as much of an impact." David Kassel, founder of ILevel, Inc., a company that specializes in providing optimal placement and secure installation of any type of artwork, agrees. He encourages his clients to group artworks on large walls. Ways to create a cohesive look with many different artworks include using the same type of frame on all pieces, keeping the measurements between the pieces the same dimension (such as two or three inches), and creating a visual centerline, a two-inch space that acts as a dado of sorts, and then hanging things above and below that void. This central axis works particularly well with different sized frames. It's important to always pick a piece that will act as an anchor, or starting point, for the arrangement. To get over any apprehension about hanging a large grouping, Kassel suggests, "You can configure your arrangement on the floor first, or cut brown paper versions of the artwork and tape it to the wall—though be aware that the art will look different once it's up."

Designers have used the grouping method in a wide variety of applications. In a sunny country kitchen, Ridder chose to hang a series of botanical prints all around the room in lieu of crown molding. For a designer show house, decorator Matthew Patrick Smyth filled an entire wall with etchings of Paris, creating a dramatic visual presentation. Smyth cautions homeowners when hanging a large grouping: "You can fill a wall with a series of prints or photographs, but I would say take care to balance the rest of the room. You do not want to end up with a lopsided space—a heavy statement on one wall, while the remaining walls are weak." In his show house

MORE ART QUESTIONS

Before buying any art, answer the following questions to know what your priorities are:

- Are you interested in art for aesthetic purposes, as an investment, or as something to fill the wall?

- What's your budget, and how will it be divided among major and minor rooms?

- What rooms have priority?

- Do you care if the walls are bare until the perfect piece is found?

- What should the art theme be (e.g., botanical prints, nudes, contemporary scenics)?

By using the same frame and similar spacing between all of the prints, designers can make many small artworks read as one large unit. Designed by Nancy Corzine.

TOP A large, bold, contemporary painting not only fills up the vast expanse of wall in a room with tall ceilings, but also adds a splash of vibrant color. Designed by Katie Ridder and Peter Pennoyer. BOTTOM Not every room requires substantial artwork. A children's bathroom is the perfect place to experiment with colorful art alternatives. Designed by Ann Fitzpatrick Brown.

design, Smyth balanced the etchings by hanging a sizable painting over the fireplace on the opposite wall, as well as designing grand curtain treatments for the window wall. Smyth also believes that you don't have to hang things floor to ceiling in a large space: "There's nothing wrong with a painting hung low above a seating group. You don't have to fill up the walls necessarily."

ART ALTERNATIVES

Fine art isn't the only solution for adding interest to a large expanse of wall. Interior designer Jamie Gibbs says, "Not every client is in the market for a Magritte or Schnabel original, and not every room calls for important art. Prints and art posters are often wonderful finishing touches." Kassel concurs: "Many people have the goal of filling a wall without spending a lot of money. And in a large house, even filling the walls with inexpensive items can add up." Kassel, who has a master's in fine art and is a practicing artist, is full of suggestions for fine art alternatives. His list of things to display includes fabric such as batiks or other handmade textiles, tapestries, screens, ethnic art such as African masks or mud cloths, any sort of collection from fish decoys to porcelain, family photographs, sconces (they don't even have to be electrified), prints and old bookplates. One item you won't find on Kassel's list, though, is posters. "If you must keep that poster from college," he advises, "hang it in the garage or mud room." Kassel reminds people to keep an open mind about what might look good on the wall, because you can find workable solutions anywhere and everywhere, including trips abroad, flea markets, thrift stores, antique shows and your grandmother's closet.

Ridder believes that art is the most important thing in an interior, but admits that it's also the most

difficult thing for her to get clients to buy. Thinking outside of the box, Ridder has hung a wide variety of decorative objects on the walls, including both found objects, such as architectural elements, and custom fabrications. "I'm fond of sticking things on the wall; it adds interest, and you can do it with any sort of budget," she explains. In a California dining room, Ridder papered the walls in silver leaf with a geometric pattern, then hung a metal, sun-shaped architectural object in the center of each square. No other art was required. In another project, Ridder worked with a craftsman to create flowers modeled out of plaster that she applied in a pattern on the wall. The result is a whimsical, one-of-a-kind powder room. If the client is more traditional, and the budget doesn't allow for fine art, Ridder turns to the magic of mirrors. "When I can't convince my clients to purchase art, I use mirrors, because they are inexpensive, and you can make them huge."

MIRROR, MIRROR

Many designers share Ridder's enthusiasm for mirrors, citing a number of positive attributes in addition to cost, including durability, flexibility and ease of use. Working on a project in Palm Beach, designer Benjamin Noriega-Ortiz

Art can substitute for architectural solutions. In this sunny kitchen, botanical prints serve in place of an elaborate cornice molding. Designed by Katie Ridder and Peter Pennoyer.

Handmade plaster flowers adhered to colorfully painted
walls are all the art needed in this long, narrow powder room.
The same technique can be used in larger rooms with equal
success. Designed by Katie Ridder and Peter Pennoyer.

placed a mirror over a large mantel. Above the mantel is a
typical place for a painting, but only a hearty oil painting
will suffice, as other works on paper would be damaged by
the heat and smoke. Often today's interiors, and today's
budgets, don't allow for a large-scale oil painting, and the
perfect substitute is a mirror. As he recalls, "There was a
built-in existing border above the fireplace—the perfect
place for a huge, formal portrait of someone the client didn't
know, but I chose to put a mirror instead. Mirrors work so
much better in a sunny climate. An oil painting would have
been too heavy, too dark."

In fact, Noriega-Ortiz is fond of using mirrors,
and does in many circumstances. "When I am afraid of
what a client will do with art, or if they don't have any art,
I usually hang a mirror." In a Park Avenue dining room
over a very grand fireplace, Noriega-Ortiz installed a large-
scale mirror. He explains: "The mantel was so big that
whatever we hung over it would have been looming over
the people sitting at the dining table. When hanging art, I
like it to be at eye-level. I always hang things lower rather
than higher. Maybe it's because I am short, but I think it's a
good general rule." Kassel agrees, saying that people tend to
look down rather than up. But if you can't hang something
at eye-level, he suggests a mirror is a wonderful solution:
"Mirrors can be hung higher than normal, because when
you see your reflection, it appears at eye-level."

Mirrors work well as artwork in a room that has a
prominent pattern on the wall, such as a mural or a scenic
wallpaper. Kassel says he always cautions his clients
against hanging anything with a motif over a highly
patterned wallpaper, instead recommending a reflective
mirror. "Scenic wallpapers are so literal, you have to be
careful what you cover." According to Kassel, another
benefit of a mirror's reflective properties is that it visually

By reflecting whatever is hung across the room, mirrors work effectively to "double" the amount of art. Designed by Lang/Robertson.

doubles the amount of fine art in a room—an important trick when attempting to fill up walls on a limited budget.

ARTFUL DISPLAY

How artwork is displayed will greatly affect the overall look of the room, as well as your ability to appreciate the art. As Kassel puts it, "The arrangement of art and objects is in itself a work of art." Through his extensive list of corporate, retail

Found objects, such as these red metal stars, can make wonderful substitutes for traditional artwork. Designed by Katie Ridder and Peter Pennoyer.

and private clients, Kassel has had the opportunity to handle a wide range of artwork, including both two-dimensional and three-dimensional pieces, such as prints, paintings, photographs, sculpture, mirrors, textiles and Asian screens. "I have worked with every type of artwork, from lunch boxes to antique barometers, in every venue."

Kassel says the actual job of hanging or installing is very quick. It's placement that takes up to 80 percent of a project's time. "My job is to help the client select the best

"The arrangement of art and objects is
in itself a work of art." — DAVID KASSEL

possible grouping of pieces, and consider how the arrangement of art complements the other design elements in the space." He claims the best way to hang art is to hire an impartial person who can look at the space with a fresh eye. "An art installer has the benefit of never having been in the space before. He can look beyond the obvious to select the most appealing place to display art."

Though he recommends using an art installer, Kassel also admits anyone can attempt the process. He suggests leaning the potential artwork up against the intended wall, and living with it there for a day or two, to make sure it works with the space. Another tip before doing the actual hanging is to fashion a brown paper mock-up and affix it with blue tape (to protect walls) to get a sense of the size and location.

PROTECTING ART

There are many factors to consider when placing art: light conditions, the style and color scheme of the décor, the other artwork in the space, the scale of the room in relation to the size of the piece, etc. However, when attempting to protect the art, the most important factor to consider is the amount of daylight in a room. This will influence what type of art is suitable. For example, delicate screens, textiles or photographs should not be in direct sunlight, unless they're protected by UV3 Plexiglas, while oil paintings are more durable and can withstand the light. Some designers recommend that clients use protective UV film, made by 3M, on the windows, particularly if the space has floor-to-ceiling glazing and/or no curtain treatments. The investment will help to protect more than the art, extending the life of all decorative objects in the room, including fabric, carpet, wallpaper, etc.

In this large room in Miami, an over-sized mirror keeps the interior light and airy. Also, a mirror makes sense over a mantel, as it can withstand the heat and smoke from the fireplace. Designed by Benjamin Noriega-Ortiz.

Delicate works on paper, such as this Asian screen, should not be in direct sunlight. This screen was hung on the wall, rather than placed on the floor, to protect it from being damaged or knocked over. Designed by Tonin MacCallum.

ACCESSORIES AND COLLECTIBLES

Like paintings and works of art, accessories should be grouped together to be effective in a large space. One of Noriega-Ortiz's clients was an avid collector of small items. He advised her to use a tray as a means of framing the collectibles. "This allows her to concentrate all her little things into one area, so they don't get lost dotted around the room," he says. Noriega-Ortiz treated some of this client's smaller prints in a similar fashion, leaning them up against the wall on side tables. "Rather than hanging them on the wall where they would have disappeared, I placed them on tables. This is much more intimate—you can pick them up and get a closer look."

Other designers also work with their clients to display accessories in a cohesive fashion. "I try to put all of the accessories together," Ridder says. "I just try to consolidate." For large collections, she recommends designing some sort of case or custom shelving unit, which can coordinate with the interior design. "You can line the back with wallpaper, use a decorative paint finish, mirror it—the options are endless." Interior designer Noel Jeffrey often incorporates a client's collection into the overall scheme of a room, constructing elaborate built-ins to house everything from French dinner plates to antique medicine bottles. For a more modern aesthetic, Peter Pennoyer designed a glass case complete with fiber optic lighting to highlight a collection of spurs and saddles. "The spurs didn't look good just lying around," he says.

OTHER ARRANGEMENTS

Plants and flowers are another way to cozy up a large interior. Large plants and potted trees allude to nature, provide dashes of calming green, and can fill up empty corners. Floral arrangements soften the lines of a space,

adding fragrance and a sense of romance. Dried grasses or branches offer unusual configurations, while being cost-effective and longer lasting.

Garden designer Rebecca Cole likes to bring green indoors, but she isn't traditional in her approach. "I'm a little odd in that I don't like tropical plants inside, unless you live in a tropical locale—then I think they're fabulous." She uses cut flowers, or flowering herbs, potted trees or perennials. "I love perennials indoors. I know they're not going to grow back next year, but they will last up to six weeks." In a big space, Cole recommends making a bold statement by using big elements such as nubby eucalyptus pods or dry bear grass. She explains, "Bear grass, 10 feet tall in a pot, would be fantastic. You never have to water it, and it's got this beautiful flow, like a waterfall. What a great motif for a contemporary space."

What's on the walls and how it is arranged makes a statement. This red bedroom has a country feel that is accentuated by the rag dolls and quilted hangings. Designed by David Bell.

Rather than hang an oil painting or a large mirror over a mantel in a New York dining room, Noriega-Ortiz collaborated with a florist to create a six-foot-tall arrangement of freshly cut, green, leafy branches. "In this room there was nothing on the ceiling, and no large paintings on the wall, so I thought this dramatic arrangement would work to capture the attention, and fill up the space. And it feels comfortable, like it would in nature, with leaves over your head." In fact, Noriega-Ortiz delivers all of his finished projects to the clients with flowers. "We like to show them what sort of floral arrangements would work in the space—what scale, what color, what type of flowers." In large spaces, Noriega-Ortiz encourages his clients to use big, bold arrangements, with colors that harmonize with the interior.

INSTALLATION

Expert installer David Kassel shares some of his industry insight:

When hanging paintings or other two-dimensional art, Kassel recommends using "D rings," one on each side of the back of the piece. This method keeps the item from shifting once it is hung. For additional security, Kassel often uses two "L brackets" (which can be painted to match the color of the wall) attached to the bottom of the frame to "lock" the painting to the wall. Still, he's quick to point out that this method only prevents casual theft, and protects items from falling due to shifts, such as mild earthquakes or rambunctious children. "The brackets are only as strong as the wallboard," says Kassel.

For installing unframed fabrics, textiles or tapestries, Kassel recommends using industrial Velcro®, with the sticky side applied to the wall, and the furry side

TOP Collections are shown to their best advantage when they are concentrated in one area, such as these blue and white ceramics in a built-in shelving unit. Designed by Diane Durell.

BOTTOM The taller spaces on the lower bookshelves create a unique place for photographs. They can also be easily changed to display other pieces from the owners' collection. Designed by Benjamin Noriega-Ortiz.

A large arrangement of green, leafy branches graces this mantel as a creative alternative to the standard mirror or oil painting. Designed by Benjamin Noriega-Ortiz.

Flowers complement art, adding a sense of freshness and youthfulness—a wonderful way to warm up any interior. Designed by Noel Jeffrey.

INSIDE FENG SHUI

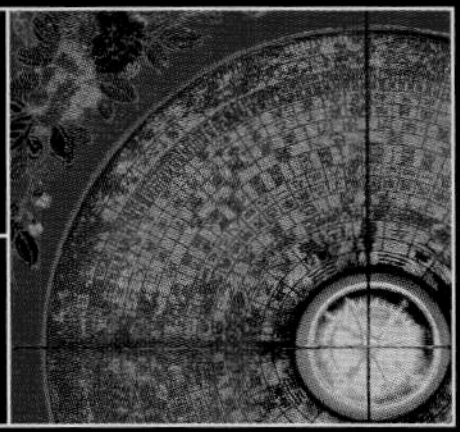

BY BENJAMIN HUNTINGTON

ART WITH FENG SHUI

The art we choose for our homes, and where we position each piece, tells people who we are and gives clues to our character. The Feng Shui interpretation of this can be very complex and is unique for each home. Below is a simple summary of each facet of our lives and how to locate it in a room. These areas sometimes change, and you have to make your own judgments about the appropriateness of each piece and where it should be positioned in your home.

The areas of our life in our home:

DREAMS & GOALS

Images and icons that are placed in the center of the wall facing people when they enter a home or room tend to reflect our directions in life. For example, a painting in a person's home of a wide-open pastoral scene with a mountain in the background would indicate that he or she was enjoying life and had some definite goals in mind.

WISDOM

This area is in the nearest left corner of any room, as seen standing at the entry door, and will show visitors how we understand and interpret the world around us.

SELF & CAREER

This area traditionally is the entry door to the space but has evolved into being in the middle of the wall where the entry door is located. Any icons in this area reflect how we see ourselves as part of the world outside our home.

COMPASSION, HELPFULNESS

This area is immediately to the right as one enters any space, and the image here reflects what sort of welcome we would give to people entering our home.

COMMUNITY & FAMILY

This area is in the center of the left wall, and images hung here reflect our connection to the communities and family that we interact with on a regular basis.

LEGACY & CREATIVITY

Here, in the center of the right-hand wall of a room, we show people what we feel we can offer the world around us.

POWER & WEALTH

This is the far left corner of the room, and the symbols here reflect a person's understanding of his or her personal power.

RELATIONSHIPS

This area is the back right-hand corner of a room, and the symbols and icons here reflect the status of our current relationships, including those with lovers, siblings, parents and children.

Take care to install your art securely and in a complementary setting. Designed by Katie Ridder and Peter Pennoyer.

stitched along the top of the textile. "Be very careful when applying the Velcro®—the sticky side is *very* sticky. My advice is to go slowly; removing it could take the paint off the wall. The stitching is easy. Use a loose, long stitch—even a corner dry cleaner could probably do it." However, if the textile in question is valuable, framing would be a better option.

In addition to shelves or tabletops, collections can be displayed on wall wedges, or architectural corbels. To keep objects safely on the wedges, Kassel uses mortician's wax. "If you want something more permanent than that, I would suggest using double-sided foam tape, but it's practically impossible to take off."

INSTALLATION FORMULA

1. Pick a Center Height
The standard center height at which items are hung is usually between 57 and 62 inches, or at eye level.

2. Start the Formula
Measure the height of the picture. Halve that dimension (divide by two). Subtract the distance from the top of the picture to one of the D-rings, or other hanging apparatus (hook, picture wire, etc.). Add the center height (57 to 62 inches).

3. Hang the Artwork
The resulting number is the height at which the hook should be placed on the wall, measured from the floor. (If using D-rings, one on each side of the picture, the two hooks should be appropriately spaced on the wall, and leveled.)

Example:
Center height: 60 inches from floor
Height of picture: 30 inches
Divide by two: 15 inches
Subtract distance from top of picture to D-ring: 6 inches
Add center height: 60 inches
$30 \div 2 = 15 - 6 = 9 + 60 = 69$
Install hooks at 69 inches above the floor.

PUNCH LIST

- ☐ Decorative and fine art objects contribute to an interior's character and color scheme, as well as give insight into your personality.

- ☐ Paintings and artwork give quality, accessories give personality and mirrors give depth.

- ☐ First assess what type of art you own, and what your budget will be for items that need to be bought.

- ☐ When purchasing fine art, develop trusted relationships with experts—art advisors, galleries, dealers and auction houses—as art is a highly complicated field.

- ☐ Consider the many alternatives to fine art, including textiles, tapestries, screens, ethnic art, collections of similar items, family photographs, sconces, prints and bookplates.

- ☐ Mirrors are one of the most cost-effective and flexible solutions to filling large walls.

- ☐ Select art based on several key factors: scale of room, quality of light, style of décor and compatibility with any existing artwork.

- ☐ If the scale of your art is too small for the scale of the room, consider grouping similar items for display.

- ☐ Keep grouped artwork cohesive by using similar frames, or keeping the spacing between the frames consistent.

- ☐ Group accessories for display; house them in appropriate shelving or display cases, or on a designated tabletop.

- ☐ Flowers and other plantings can be used indoors to soften an interior. The style and scale of arrangements should reflect the interior and locality.

The artwork in this foyer complements all the other elements in the design scheme. Lighting a work of art dramatically can make it too prominent, distracting the eye from the room's other beautiful accoutrements. Designed by Katie Ridder and Peter Pennoyer.

CHAPTER 8

ILLUMINATION
THE WELL-LIT CHALLENGE

Just as the walls, furnishings and art need to be thoughtfully planned , the quality of light in your large home needs to be carefully considered. David Easton believes that poorly-lit rooms lose their allure. "It is much easier to enjoy a room

that exudes luminous ambiance than a room that's awash in glare, or shrouded in shadows," he says. Creating a lighting system for your home is considerably more complex than simply selecting light fixtures. By planning carefully, incorporating your family's lifestyle and activities, and defining the moods you'd like to create, you'll be able to achieve a functional, flexible and comfortable lighting system throughout your home.

LIGHTING REQUIREMENTS

Regardless of whether yours is a household of six or just a bachelor pad, the task of lighting your house begins with an understanding of who lives there and what their lifestyle requires. "I try to create a lighting scheme that relates to the people who will be living in a home," says lighting designer Bill Schwinghammer. "I ask about their habits and how they think about their homes."

Matthew Patrick Smyth agrees and says that he tries to be as specific as possible with lighting questions during initial interviews: "I try to work with my clients to figure out where they think they will do most of their tasks, such as reading, so I can determine the areas of the house that will need strong light." Smyth recommends asking yourself questions including some of the following: Where will you sit in the afternoon? How are you going to entertain? What activities will take place in each room, and

where? "For example, if you know you're going to put a bed on a particular wall, you'll want to make sure you have lamplight on each side," he advises. "Over by the fireplace, where you will likely sit and read, make sure there are ample outlets for lighting."

Each room requires a unique lighting composition to make it warm, inviting and functional. Designed by Eric Cohler.

THE INVERSE SQUARE

Using an equation called the "inverse square law," experts demonstrate that as you raise a light fixture, the beam of light widens and becomes more dispersed. For example, take the average light fixture hanging in an average room with eight-foot ceilings. If you now take the same fixture and hang it in a room with double-height ceilings, say 16 feet high, rather than receiving half the amount of light from the beam of light, you will only receive a quarter.

Equation: X^2 (original distance away, squared) divided by Y^2 (further distance away, squared), multiplied by 100 = percentage of original brightness.

Example: 8^2 (64) divided by 16^2 (256), multiplied by 100 = 25%

A home is an assortment of moods. Plan carefully so that your design will reflect those moods perfectly. Designed by Frank Geary Designs.

To create a lighting system that truly fits your lifestyle, architect Monique Corbat Brooks and designer Alicia Ritts Orrick, who work together, advise that furniture and lighting plans must be done in tandem (See Chapter 6, *Decorating Details*, for more information). "You can't do a correct lighting plan without a furniture plan," says Orrick. "What happens so often is that architects will design a house not knowing where any furniture will be placed, and they light the space in general. This causes problems, because the light won't always be where you need it to be."

Manhattan lighting designer Lewis Herman, who

has a degree in psychology, says, "What I do for a living isn't about quantifying how many watts go into how many square feet, or how many foot-candles light up a room; it's truly about treating each person as an individual in order to see what will make them absolutely love their home. It's not just about walking into a room and turning on a switch; it's about making magic."

COMPLEX LIGHT FORMS

One of the greatest challenges in lighting a home is that each and every room requires a unique lighting composition to achieve the best possible effect. Lighting large rooms presents even greater challenges, because when ceiling heights rise and spaces expand, the light that illuminates the room must work harder to do so effectively and comfortably (see "The Inverse Square" sidebar). Schwinghammer advises that every space should be approached as if you're orchestrating a composition of light, harmoniously blending up light, down light and diffuse light through a variety of forms including ambient, task and accent (see "Lighting Defined" sidebar). "An expert once told me that to have a successfully lit large space you need thirty-two different sources of light," recalls interior designer Miles Redd. "I found that interesting, so I tried it. I designed a room that had literally thirty-two sources—several five-watt picture lights, a couple of ceiling fixtures, pairs of table lamps, several task lights, and up lights in all the corners. Surprisingly, it was very soothing." While this specific number and combination of fixtures will not work for every space, the challenge remains the same: how to combine a variety of fixtures without over- or under-lighting the space.

Lighting designer Carl Hillmann says that nature may be the best teacher where lighting is concerned.

"Think of the sun and its different incarnations throughout the day—the soft glow of sunrise, the glare of high noon and the long shadows of sunset," Hillmann says, adding that like the sun, light fixtures can re-create a wide variety of scenarios when carefully combined. "Each period of day has its own characteristics and colors. Just as nature has its various moods, houses do as well," he explains. "There is the time when only the two of you are at home; there is the dinner with a few friends; and then there is the big party or grand business function. All of those situations have different feelings and require different lighting

LIGHTING DEFINED

Accent Lighting: Specific, narrow-focus light that dramatically highlights particular objects. Example: Pin-light on sculpture or artwork.

Ambient Lighting: General artificial lighting that compensates for lack of natural light and provides uniform illumination. Example: A ceiling fixture hung in the middle of a room.

Diffused Lighting: Light that is distributed in every direction, creating a uniform glow. Example: A translucent globe.

Down Lighting: Fixtures that project light downward, towards the lower part of the room and onto horizontal surfaces such as seating, counters and tabletops.

Light Cove: A shelf that is built out near the ceiling plane. Lights are often placed on top of the shelf in order to up-light the ceiling.

Recessed Lighting (Architectural Lighting): Fixtures that recess behind the ceiling plane. Example: A car headlight.

Sconces: Light fixtures that are mounted on the wall, and wired into the electrical system of a house.

Small Aperture Lighting: Designer-friendly architectural lighting—small, round recessed fixtures that are inserted into the ceiling, such as MR-16s, which have an aperture of about two inches—much smaller than early fixtures.

Task Lighting: Bright, concentrated light directed down onto a limited area, illuminating a specific task. Example: A desk lamp, or recessed fixture over kitchen sink.

Up Lighting: Fixtures that project light upwards, towards the upper part of the room or the ceiling.

This room successfully layers light, from the chandelier on the ceiling, to the sconces on the wall, to the candles on the horizontal surfaces, and finally, to the fireplace at floor level. Designed by Carleen Murdock.

LIGHT LAYERS

If the fixtures are the ingredients in our lighting system recipe, you need to determine the number and type you need, as well as a method for successfully combining them. According to the experts, the most flexible and comprehensive system will include four layers of light: recessed, or architectural, lighting located behind the ceiling plane (can lights, eyeball fixtures); drop-down ceiling fixtures (chandeliers, lanterns, track lighting or cove lighting); wall-mounted fixtures (sconces and picture lights) and occasional lighting (floor and table lamps).

options. To have a comfortable home, it is important to have a lighting system that is flexible."

TAKE IT FROM THE TOP

When figuring out the best combination of lighting fixtures, the experts tend to start from the ceiling plane and work their way down. Recessed lighting, such as can lights and eyeball fixtures, are typically used for task-oriented down lighting. High-end designers recommend using these types of fixtures with restraint, as there are significant potential drawbacks.

"Recessed lighting, especially if used with abandon, can kill ambiance, regardless of how well the interiors have been designed," says Easton. "Down lighting is unattractive because it throws deep shadows on people's faces. And it loses the sense of mystery and drama by obliterating the chiaroscuro—the interplay of light and shade—in the space." Hillmann elaborates on Easton's theory. "When designing your lighting scheme," he says, "the ultimate goal is to make people, artwork and furniture look as good as they possibly can. Ideally, beams of light shouldn't illuminate people; they should light objects. Use recessed and other accent lighting to highlight your objects in a dramatic way or bring them out subtly in the background."

Eyeball and can lights also run the risk of creating unsightly interruptions in the ceiling plane, or, even worse, looking like gaping holes in tall spaces. "The higher the fixture is mounted," Hillman explains, "the more readily you're going to be able to see up into it. A fixture that is well shielded in an 8-foot ceiling is glary in a 12-foot ceiling." To minimize this effect, many lighting companies have developed fixtures with small apertures, such as MR-16s. The benefit to using these smaller fixtures is the ability to provide down light from much less conspicuous sources. When specifying lighting, top interior designers such as Redd and Zina Glazebrook use MR-16s in limited applications. Redd will generally place down lights in each corner of a room. "This prevents those areas from appearing dark and uninviting," he says. Glazebrook likes to use MR-16s in the kitchen. "I love them because they are so small," she remarks. "I place them in a checkerboard pattern, which is more interesting than putting them in straight rows."

Architects also see the benefits to certain inconspicuous recessed fixtures. Peter Pennoyer likes to use trimless Nulux fixtures; he admires their beauty and functionality. "They can be purchased as recessed, recessed linear or as track lighting. And like MR-16s, the apertures are small, making the architectural fixtures aesthetically appropriate for homes." Schwinghammer also recommends going trimless. "In residential interiors,

RECIPES FOR LIGHTING

Living Room
Layered light in the living room: recessed light for art; table and floor lamps for tasks; and cove lighting for ambiance.

Dining Room
Wall sconces and a chandelier or hanging fixture create the right mix.

Kitchen
Task lighting is ultra important. Place light sources below and above cabinets to provide ample light. Placing a fixture over the sink is also recommended. Everything on dimmers, say experts.

Bathroom
Light the vanity and the bathtub/shower separately. And, as in the rest of the house, dimmers will help you adjust the mood in the bathroom from romantic to task-oriented.

Bedroom
Place ambient ceiling fixtures for dressing, as well as task lighting for the closet and for the bedside for reading.

THE COLOR OF LIGHT

The gases in a bulb react to the electrical current passing through, resulting in different qualities and colors.

Incandescent Tungsten:
Continuous spectral distribution that emits a warm light similar to sunlight or candlelight. Due to the warm glow, interiors will appear more yellow than they are. Drawbacks: Short life span, and loss of brightness with age.

Full Spectrum: An incandescent bulb that emits a whiter, truer light, more representational of sunlight—excellent for combating seasonal disorders. Drawbacks: More expensive than regular incandescent bulbs, but longer lasting.

Fluorescent: Cool white light with blue cast. More expensive to install, but much more energy efficient and cost effective over the long term; it lasts ten times longer than incandescent tungsten, and emits three times more light for equivalent wattage. Drawbacks: Can seem unnatural; can only be used for ambient lighting; hard to dim. Sometimes hums when dimmed.

Halogen (incandescent quartz):
Whiter, more intense light than incandescent tungsten—except when dimmed. Dimming halogen light brings the color temperature down and creates a warmer glow. These fixtures are smaller and more energy efficient. Drawbacks: Intense heat and high glare.

If you must use recessed, architectural lighting fixtures in a residential setting, make sure they have small apertures, and combine them with other fixtures, such as sconces. Designed by Sidnam Petrone Gartner.

I almost always plaster the fixtures in and paint them to match the color of the ceiling," he explains. "Architectural fixtures really don't belong in a house, so you've got to paint over them to make them as unobtrusive as possible."

Schwinghammer prefers to avoid recessed halogen light in residential settings, but will occasionally use low-voltage halogen lamps (MR-16s). "The issue with halogen fixtures in a home is that halogen light is very white," he says. "Compared to incandescent light sources—table and floor lamps, pendants and chandeliers, which have a warm color temperature—halogen feels brighter. It's difficult to create an intimate and warm environment with it because it is such a modern light source."

"If you must incorporate architectural lighting into a room," says Pennoyer, "you should absolutely spend the money to hire a professional lighting designer." Pennoyer routinely works with Hillmann, who does both residential projects and commercial work, such as museum collections and exhibitions. "Even though you may say, 'I know what I want: I want these two walls to be evenly lit,' hiring a lighting designer gives you the advantage of having someone calculate exactly how many inches away from the walls the fixtures should be, and what kind of light bulbs they should have in them," explains Pennoyer. "Then the designer can come back after the lights are installed and focus and adjust them to ensure that they function as desired."

Pennoyer adds, "Even when clients and designers know they want Nulux light, or Edison Price lights, or whatever the top lights are, that is still just the beginning. Those lights are so expensive that it is really worth having someone calculate, so that you don't have scallops on the wall or the client isn't surprised, saying, 'Oh, the halogen light is too white and commercial for my house.'" Pennoyer says that even though hiring a lighting designer means another fee, it will make a substantial difference in whether you're able to achieve the effect you envision. "It's very tempting not to involve another person because the process of building or renovating is already complicated enough, but it really is worth it in the end."

DROP-DOWN LIGHTING

The next layer of light in a room is created by fixtures that drop down from the ceiling—pendants, chandeliers and track lighting—or fixtures that meld with the architecture, such as cove lighting.

When rooms are tall, experts agree that you need to illuminate the ceiling. "You really must get some light up high so that your space doesn't go up into darkness," says Hillmann. "If you have that much space, you want to

ASSESS YOUR LIGHTING NEEDS

- Do I want a whole-house system? Where would dimmer switches be useful?

- How much natural light is there from windows, glass doors and skylights?

- Do I have lighting situations in my home now that I could learn from, to either achieve the same effect if I like it or prevent it from happening again if I don't?

- Which direction does the new home face and which areas will need more light due to an absence of natural light?

- How can I orient the new addition to my home to take more advantage of natural light?

- How will I use each room?

- Do I want to read or use my computer in this room? Do I need specific task lighting? If so, where?

- Will I want to entertain in this room? If so, do I want to be able to dramatically increase or decrease the amount of light when guests are visiting?

- Do I want to create a romantic feel in this room?

- Do I want my artwork or collectibles to really stand out or to be more subtly lit?

- Where will the furniture be placed and how will that affect the lighting plan?

- Where will my artwork and collectibles be displayed?

Using recessed lighting to illuminate architectural features, such as this fireplace and these columns, provides adequate light without causing glare. Designed by Russell Eppright Custom Homes.

Drop-down ceiling fixtures can be sculptural as well as functional. This designer decided to go one step further by draping the fixtures in gauzy fabric to add a sense of warmth to the interior. Designed by Benjamin Noriega-Ortiz.

see it and appreciate it." Drop-down ceiling fixtures are an excellent way of directing light up onto the overhead plane. With their wide variety of styles, pendants can emit diffused light, up light, down light or a combination. It is possible to have too much of a good thing, though; Hillmann cautions: "Be careful that you don't overdo it and have too much light going up, or you might turn the space upside down."

One way to ensure that you don't overdo it is to hire a lighting consultant to incorporate lighting into the architecture. Much like recessed lighting, cove lighting must be well thought out and addressed in the planning stages of your design. A cove can be built anywhere the planes of the room intersect; it is essentially a pocket or cornice that runs the length of the wall, or walls, that the track is tucked into. Lighting experts tout the benefits of cove lighting because it is a very sophisticated system that is infinitely flexible. The same track can accommodate wall washers, or accent lights, or a combination of wide and narrow beams. However, the most common use of coves is to gently wash soft, indirect, ambient light over walls or ceilings. "Coves can be designed so that you're hardly aware of where the light is coming from—all you see is softly glowing architecture," Hillmann says.

In addition to up lighting, chandeliers, lanterns and other centrally located hanging fixtures serve other functions. "Not only do pendant fixtures light an interior," says Easton, "but they also serve as sculptural objects in a room, emphasizing the scale of a space." Redd also values ceiling fixtures in large rooms with high ceilings. "A chandelier or lantern will help lift the eye up. It's a focal point, a decorative object," he explains. "I like to place ceiling fixtures over a table or significant seating area, because it draws attention to what's underneath it."

Though not as prevalent in high-end residential projects, track lighting is probably the most flexible drop-down ceiling option for the least amount of money, as the track can be installed and fixtures can be added or subtracted at any given time. Style can be flexible as well, since both modern and traditional fixtures can be attached. If you are designing on a budget, this system is a very good idea.

UP AGAINST THE WALL

The third layer of lighting involves fixtures that are mounted directly onto the wall, namely sconces and picture lights. These types of fixtures placed thoughtfully around a room

Decorative wall sconces are a wonderful way to add ambient light to an interior. Designed by Noel Jeffrey.

will help to infuse soft spots of ambient or accent lighting. These types of lights are rarely if ever used for task lighting—the wattage is usually low, and the location of the fixtures too distant from task areas. (The exception is the swing-arm reading lamp, which is usually wall-mounted, one on either side of the bed, or above a seating area.)

Katie Ridder is a big fan of sconces, citing their decorative properties and ease of use. She says they are marvelous ways to add additional sources of light without risking over-lighting a room. "In the ballroom of a country house Peter Pennoyer and I designed, we used a great number of sconces, ten in all, to set the tone," she says. "The light from sconces is soft and ambient. They don't really run the risk of making the room too bright."

Traditional picture lights lend a sort of old world charm to an interior. Typically made of brass and fitted with five-watt bulbs, picture lights glow softly above a painting. However, there are drawbacks to these low-tech fixtures, namely the inability to control the beam, which leads to scallops of light illuminating a portion of the

Properly lighting an art collection can make a big difference in how a room feels. Experts say that art should not stand alone, but should blend beautifully with the design scheme of the room. Designed by Hariette Levine.

artwork, while the rest is bathed in shadows. For the avid and sophisticated collector, new developments and high-tech fixtures are available (see "Illuminating Art," later in this chapter).

FILLING IN: FLOOR AND TABLE LAMPS

Floor and table lamps, the next layer of lighting, help bring the lighting down to a human level. Most of this lighting is at eye level or below. Lamps serve a variety of functions, providing both ambient and task lighting. Table lamps offer the perfect accompaniment to seating groups or areas of activity, such as desks or game tables, while floor lamps or torchiers tuck neatly into corners.

"Lamps are incredibly sophisticated lighting instruments," says Hillmann. "The classic lamp with a base and shade provides pretty strong light down, some light up, and what comes out horizontally to light you is diffused and softened by the shade. That is very sophisticated and has never needed improving. And while the basics are always the same, there are endless variations and all kinds of different styles. This makes lamps very formidable lighting tools."

Smyth believes a significant portion of the overall light in a home, even in a large one, should be lamplight. "Having those warm pools of light is important," he explains. "These spots make a room inviting and comforting." A home he designed in Sagaponack, New York, had a living room with a very high ceiling, which peaked at twenty feet. "That was a challenge because we didn't want a lot of overhead light; you'd see the glaring bulbs with a ceiling that high," says Smyth. "I used fifteen lamps in the room to make it feel very inviting. The lamplight also brought the level of light down to a more

Eye-level light sources are important in a room when ceilings are high, especially in areas where tasks are performed. Designed by Anthony Antine.

personal level. It's all eye level when you walk into a room instead of above, so it feels much more intimate."

Unlike other lighting, which must be planned in advance, lamps can be added at any time. All you need to do is plug them in. The only advance planning suggestion is to make sure you have enough outlets in convenient locations. "Having ample outlets is especially challenging in large rooms," Smyth remarks. "So many of the newer homes have big rooms with lots of windows and entryways and no walls, so most of the furniture has to float in the middle of the room. I think a very important point in planning lighting in these rooms is to incorporate floor outlets, because you don't want people to trip over extension cords or to have wires running across the room."

TASK-ORIENTED LIGHTING

Lighting in those rooms where the tasks are very specific— the kitchen and the bathrooms—is one area where many experts relax their views about recessed lighting, since it's important for the light in these spaces to be bright, but not glaring.

Hillmann cautions that a kitchen should provide adequate light without being overwhelming. "If you light a project at a commercial level, you'll drive people out of the house," he says. He points to restaurants that are lit so dramatically that there's glare on the soup. Though direct lighting on countertops where food will be prepared is necessary, a bright light over a table is not a good idea unless a dimmer switch will allow the light to be softened at meal times. Smyth agrees for several reasons. "It's very important to be able to dim all the kitchen lights when you're serving dinner, even if you're eating in the adjoining dining room," he explains. "Nothing breaks the

TOP Care should be taken when lighting kitchens; tasks there require brighter light than in other rooms in the home. Designed by Sidnam Petrone Gartner. BOTTOM Dimmers are important where light levels need to shift subtly for ambiance, such as the dining room during mealtime. Designed by Brooks & Orrick.

mood faster than having the door swing open to the dining room, which is nicely candlelit and everyone is relaxed, and have a blast of light come in from the kitchen. It's jarring and it breaks the flow of conversation."

Smyth says lighting should also be carefully considered in the pantry and bathrooms, as these are areas where you often search for things that can be difficult to find. "Many times when you walk into the bathroom to look for something, you don't have your contacts in, and you don't want to have to worry about glasses," he says. "This is why it's a good idea to make the room as bright as possible. But, again, I recommend putting every overhead fixture on a dimmer. There's nothing worse than killing a mood by having over-lit rooms, even if they are task-oriented areas."

Herman adds closets to the list of areas that require strong light. "People tend to see a room as a whole and they don't think about details," he explains. "If they want a muted light in the bedroom, they forget that they will need to be able to see whether a garment is black or blue when they open the closet door. I take ambiance into consideration, but I never forget about the functional requirements of lighting a room."

Adequate light in task-oriented areas is important to maintaining healthy eyesight (see "Tips for Maintaining Healthy Eyesight" sidebar). Light is also a recognized treatment for seasonal affective disorder (SAD), and it greatly affects the circadian rhythm in human beings, says Mariana Gross Figueiro of the Lighting Research Center in Troy, New York. The strength of the light, as well as its color, is important. Therefore, choosing light on the blue end of the spectrum rather than the red end (halogen as opposed to incandescent) is a wise choice for task-oriented areas, such as over kitchen countertops.

TIPS FOR MAINTAINING HEALTHY EYESIGHT

Kitchen
A recessed down light centered over the sink makes washing dishes and preparing food easier.

Under-cabinet lights, hidden from view, are helpful. Where tasks such as chopping are carried out, it's best to locate lighting slightly to the side and in front of the position where a person would stand while performing the task.

Bathroom
Bathroom lighting should be bright, uniform and shadow-free, with minimal glare, as good lighting is important for shaving, grooming, applying make-up, showering and reading fine print on prescription bottles.

Place a recessed, wet-location-rated down light in the ceiling above the tub, using a 52-watt halogen lamp. Switch it separately from the other lights in the room.

Bedroom
Create both low-level ambient light, for a relaxing atmosphere, and bright areas, for task-oriented activities.

Swing-arm task lights mounted on each side of the bed make reading more comfortable. The Lighting Institute recommends 18-watt/830 compact fluorescent lamps with an electronic ballast, because these lights provide adequate reading light and are environmentally friendly.

Living Room/Den
A lamp should be located behind and slightly to the side of the reader, with the shade located at eye level when a person is seated.

Use frosted lamps in light fixtures where the bulbs are visible to reduce glare. Light fixtures that completely restrict the view of the bulb are best. To test whether your home has too much glare, wear a baseball cap around the house. If you're more comfortable with the cap on, reduce the amount of glare by replacing clear bulbs with frosted ones or replacing fixtures that expose the light bulb to the naked eye. Reducing eye strain reduces tension, which supports a calmer, more pleasant and functional environment.

Home Office
Pay close attention to lighting in a home office to minimize glare on a computer screen.

Place lighting so that no shadows are created on the work plane.

ILLUMINATING ART

A significant challenge in a large interior is the proper lighting of an art collection that may contain a number of over-sized pieces. How to light these sizable works of art without interfering with the intimacy in a room is a challenge.

Art does not always need specialized lighting. When it is placed informally, such as on a side table, lamp light or ambient light is often suitable. Designed by Glenn Gissler.

Hillmann points out that well-lit artwork will create visual texture and variety in an interior. Even if a homeowner doesn't have an art collection, there's a chance a collection will develop over time, so if the home you're planning is the dream home that you expect to live in for many years, choose certain walls as gallery walls, advises Hillmann. To prevent surplus light fixtures that may never be used, Hillmann will often use a technique that's utilized in galleries. "We might put a slot in the ceiling, or we might pop the ceiling up a little—take it out from the wall before we drop it back down, which creates a coffer that is connected to the wall," he explains. "The track goes in the corner, so it's not hanging down; it's tucked in. You can put wall washers on the track or accent lights or a combination—it gives you that flexibility."

If you already have a collection, and you want to light it in a professional manner, turn to the experts. Schwinghammer, an authority on lighting art, has specified lighting for a number of museums, including the 2003 exhibition *Vincent's Choice* at the Van Gogh Museum in Amsterdam. In museum settings, he generally uses a low voltage SoLux® MR-16 lamp because it brings the color temperature up and provides the best color rendering, which makes the art "pop" off the wall. But he cautions against using this extremely white light source in a residence, even if an art collection takes center stage. "I like to keep the color temperature on the artwork low, keeping it similar to incandescence," he explains. "I think it's difficult to create an interior that is really warm and inviting and comfortable when you make the artwork jump off the wall."

Framing projectors, which are specially cut masks that fit the beam of light to the exact size of an art-work, have become popular tools for achieving a perfectly lit painting. Many lighting designers prefer them to traditional gallery lights, which don't provide an even coverage of light over the entire surface of a painting—a particular problem for the large works that often grace the walls of sizeable rooms. Though Schwinghammer uses these often in museum settings, he says the luminescence of the painting can overpower an interior setting.

"Artwork needs to contribute to the interior environment rather than stand alone," he remarks. "If you use cooler light on them, you see every color in them, and if you use framing projectors so that they're perfectly lit, you're going to make them have a life of their own. I personally think it's a bit pretentious to do that." Schwinghammer prefers controlled pools of halogen light on art, but he steers clear of wall washers because they wash the wall above a piece of art and fight with the artwork for attention. "I use controlled flooding of the painting, and because a halogen lamp has a multi-faceted reflector that throws off a stray beam pattern, which is striated and harsh, I use a piece of stippled glass that softens the beam," he says. "This softens all the shadows, and makes the light smoother and richer feeling."

Schwinghammer has helped to develop a picture light that delicately washes light over the entire surface of a painting, which he believes is a better way to light a painting than traditional gallery lights and framing projectors. The Litelab PictureWash™ fixtures, manufactured by the Litelab Corporation in Buffalo, New York, have a power supply that's fully concealed behind the artwork and can be fitted with beam-spread lenses to modify the dimensions of the light wash as artwork displays are changed. Tailored Lighting, Inc., in Rochester, New York, produces a similar fixture, the SoLux® Art Light, which uses the SoLux® Daylight Bulb.

If you choose to have a high-tech lighting system installed, always counterbalance it with subtler, more friendly lighting, such as this eye-level sconce. Designed by Eve Robinson.

LIGHTING GETS TECHNICAL

The technological advancements of the past two decades have brought the lighting industry its share of innovation. With the advent of computerized systems for the home, you can choose the moods you want your home to reflect during different times of the day and evening, and have these moods orchestrated with precision, day-in and day-out.

From a lighting scheme as simple as six bare bulbs to the most complex whole-house control systems that can be programmed to anticipate your every mood, lighting schemes often reflect a homeowner's temperament and level of patience. If you are not a technophobe, computerized systems have become ultra savvy accoutrements in home environments. Hillmann remarks that

A whole-house control system can select specific areas of this loft to illuminate, creating individual settings for morning, day and evening lighting. Designed by Scott Craven.

simple dimmers that create ambiance, and pre-set systems that borrowed techniques from the theater to pre-program certain environmental systems, such as lighting and temperature, are becoming ancient history. "Whole-house control systems are now computer-based, and you can accomplish a variety of things by touching screens or buttons," he says. "Not only do they light scenes—a term also borrowed from the theater—but they can also grab zones that you wouldn't ordinarily have as a scene, such as a path from your bedroom down to the kitchen, which could be called 'midnight snack path.'"

Schwinghammer maintains that the control system is the most challenging element in the very large

"Some of the most romantic times in the house are the transitions between daylight and darkness." — CARL HILLMANN

home. Because these systems are created specifically to affect the ambiance in each room in a home, one of the greatest challenges may be to make you comfortable with such a technologically advanced system. "The system is fine as long as the homeowner takes an interest in it and works with the person who sets the settings so that he knows what each button does," he explains. "But I've known people who have been left with systems that they find incomprehensible: it's like having a VCR that you can't program."

If you have your heart set on a system that will anticipate your every move, you should spend time with the programmer to understand what's being done, Schwinghammer suggests. This will ensure that you have a system that is manageable. Until a homeowner becomes comfortable with the operation of a whole-house system, Schwinghammer creates several scenarios that are easily changed to achieve a different mood. "I designate five different levels: low (where everything's on a low setting), medium, high, cocktail hour (which may be very dramatic) and an emergency setting (where everything is full-up)."

"Also make sure that every switch and every level in the house is written down," Schwinghammer adds. "We worked on a house where there was a flood and every-thing had to be ripped out. Fortunately, we had it all documented. There was a back-up file on a disk, but we also felt it was important to have a print-out." Schwinghammer was therefore able to reinstall the whole-house control system exactly as it had been originally. His last caveat to anyone who purchases or inherits a system? "Make sure you have a good service company in case you need them in an emergency."

Though challenging to operate, if technology is

With large houses come potentially complicated lighting systems. Be sure to understand how your system is pro-grammed and how to make any desired changes. Designed by Sidnam Petrone Gartner.

INSIDE
FENG SHUI

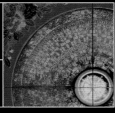

BY BENJAMIN HUNTINGTON

LIGHT

Lighting is an integral part of Feng Shui; without it we could not live. As humans we instinctually need the lighting in our environments to simulate the light and shade of nature.

LIGHTING CONCERNS

If there's too much light from overhead sources, we instinctually feel exposed (as if we're in a desert environment with no shade).

If there's too much light from one direction, our instinct will signal that we would be unable to identify danger. This gives us a feeling of uneasiness.

If there are too many dark areas in a space, our instinct will warn us of hidden dangers.

Normal electric lighting has much more yellow than natural light.

LIGHTING REMEDIES

Make sure that the lighting sources in most rooms are varied, and that at least 50 percent of the lighting is not from overhead lights. This does not apply to hallways, stairways and the entry hall, where more overhead lighting is necessary.

Use dimmer switches as much as possible. The "pre-set" type is quite useful, as you can leave them dimmed and just switch them on and off.

Make sure you have sufficient light for each space; inexpensive can up lights tucked behind a plant or piece of furniture can work wonders for a dark corner.

In important lighting areas (e.g., bedsides, reading areas and desks) use full-spectrum daylight-adjusted bulbs. They are more expensive, but they give a more natural light and last longer.

PREVIOUS PAGE Houses tend to emit light at night, causing a bit of a lantern effect. Be sure to light certain elements outside to counter it. Designed by John Gills. ABOVE To avoid creating mirrors out of your windows at night, extend your view into the landscape by lighting specific outdoor features. Designed by Robert Jackson Architects.

not your strong suit, well-programmed whole-house control systems will turn the lights on outside when darkness descends, fill the house with your favorite music and light the task-oriented areas of a home automatically at the prescribed times of the day.

EXPANDING YOUR NIGHT VIEW

When designing your lighting system don't forget to think about your rooms at all times of the day. Nighttime is a potential hazard for big spaces with large windows and lots of light fixtures. "The problem with large areas of glass is that unless you can see something through it, it's a mirror at night," explains Hillmann. "In order to feel relaxed, safe and secure, people need to be able to see what's around them."

Lighting experts say that landscape lighting is a good way to prevent windows from turning black at night. Lit trees and landscaped elements provide a view beyond the windows. Schwinghammer agrees: "In order to see through the glass at night, you've got to either have just as much light outside as you have inside, or less light inside than you have outside. If you pay for a wall of glass, you must like what's out there, so you want to be sure you can see it. Making the nighttime view available to your rooms will also make them more dynamic."

In terms of layering light, outdoor illumination is an entirely different ballgame. There is one major difference: there's no ceiling. Exterior lighting for the most part is located in the ground, or on hardscaping elements such as walkways, steps, pergolas, etc. Turn to the experts for advice on how to effectively highlight certain objects, such as trees and pools, and illuminate pathways for safe circulation.

PUNCH LIST

☐ Over-lit rooms lose their magic.

☐ Every room requires a unique lighting composition to achieve the best possible effect.

☐ Light furniture, objects and art, not people.

☐ A beautifully lit room will have four layers of light: recessed ceiling lights, drop-down ceiling fixtures, walls sconces and picture lights, and floor and table lamps.

☐ Used with abandon, recessed lighting can kill ambiance in a room.

☐ Use trimless recessed lighting for a tailored, clean aesthetic.

☐ Light sources of different temperatures create different effects.

☐ Task-oriented lighting in rooms such as kitchens and bathrooms should be bright enough to provide ample light on the work plane, but put overhead lighting in these rooms on dimmers in order to moderate the light—and the mood— in the room.

☐ Put as much lighting as possible on dimmers.

☐ There are a variety of tools for accomplishing the perfect lighting of an art collection, including framing projectors, filters and lenses. Experts advise that artwork should contribute to the interior environment of a home rather than stand alone.

☐ Whole-house control systems can create a variety of moods at the flick of a button.

☐ To have a nighttime view, you have to have just as much light outside as you have inside. Install landscape lighting to introduce light into your outdoor spaces.

RESOURCES

Resources are one of the most important aspects of interior design and architecture. There are literally tens of thousands of vendors, artisans, suppliers, manufacturers and retailers out there. In this appendix, you'll find a selection of the

Garden designers, architects, lighting specialists and interior designers are just a few of the components required to create a successful project—you'll also need to know where to buy products, artworks and other important materials. Designed by Anthony Cochran.

authors' and the experts' favorites. Please note that many of the listings have multiple locations. Due to limited space, we've included the contact information for the U.S. headquarters only. Please call the vendor directly for a location or supplier near you. Also many of the sources listed sell to the trade (architects and designers) only. If you aren't working with an interior designer or architect, you may be able to get a contact number from the vendor of a design service that may purchase the items for you.

RESOURCES COVERED (IN ORDER)

Architects	Antiques
Associations	Antique Restoration
Contractors	Artisans
Interior Designers	Beds & Bedding
Landscape Architects/	Carpets & Rugs
Garden Designers	Carpet Restoration
Outdoor & Garden Furniture	Curtain Hardware & Other
Appliances	Window Specialties
Bath & Kitchen Fixtures	Fabric
Architectural Salvage	Fireplace Surrounds & Mantels
Metalwork	Furniture
Hardware Suppliers	Specialty Items
Moldings	Trimming
Tile	Upholsterers
Windows & Doors	Art Services
Wine Cellars	Auction Houses
Painters	Framing
Paint Companies/Distributors	Lampshades
Wallpaper	Lighting
Wallpaper Hangers	Lighting Designers

CHAPTER ONE: GETTING STARTED

ARCHITECTS

Catalano Architects Inc.
Thomas P. Catalano, AIA
374 Congress Street
Boston, MA 02210
T: 617.338.7447
F: 617.338.6639
www.catalanoinc.com
Architectural firm specializing in high-end residential design.

Elise Geiger Design
Elise Geiger
6 East 68th Street, Suite 1A
New York, NY 10021
T: 212.439.1985
elise@emgdesign.com
Architect and author of the upcoming Elements of Living title *The Essence of Home*, on seven essentials of home design.

John Gillis, Architect
41 East 11 Street
New York, NY 10003
T: 212.254.5010
F: 718.237.0203
jgillis@architetto.com
Specializes in architecture with modern accents.

Haverson Architecture & Design
Jay Haverson
63 Church Street
Greenwich, CT 06830
T: 203.629.8300
F: 203.629.8399
www.haversonarchitecture.com
Architectural firm specializing in high-end residential design.

Jeffrey Cole Architects
Jeffrey Cole
93 St. Marks Place, 4th Floor
New York, NY 10009
T: 212.529.7542
F: 212.473.3079
www.jeffreycolearchitects.com
Architectural firm offering innovative solutions for residential and commercial clients.

Glenn Leitch, AIA
348 West 36th Street, #8S
New York, NY 10018
T: 212.736.1574
gleitch@ha-ny.com
Architectural designs with a focus on space planning and customization.

Peter Pennoyer Architects, PPaC
Peter Pennoyer
1239 Broadway, Penthouse
New York, NY 10001
T: 212.779.9765
F: 212.779.3814
www.ppapc.com
Leading firm in classical and historically based design.

Sidnam Petrone Gartner
Coty Sidnam, Bill Petrone, Eric Gartner
136 West 21st Street
New York, NY 10011
T: 212.366.5500
F: 212.366.6559
www.spgarchitects.com
Leading firm with specialty in modern vernacular.

ASSOCIATIONS

The American Institute of Architects (AIA)
1735 New York Avenue, NW
Washington, DC 20006
T: 800.AIA.3837
F: 202.626.7547
www.aia.org
Offers architect referral services.

American Society of Interior Designers (ASID)
608 Massachusetts Avenue, NE
Washington, D.C. 20002
T: 202.546.3480
F: 202.546.3240
www.asid.org
Network of interior designers.

Appraisers Association of America
386 Park Avenue South
New York, NY 10016
T: 212.889.5404
F: 212.889.5503
www.appraisersassoc.org
Offers standards for property appraisal, as well as a database of professional appraisers.

Associated Landscape Contractors of America
150 Elden Street, Suite 270
Herndon, VA 20170
T: 800.395.ALCA
or 703.736.9666
F: 703.736.9668
www.alca.org
Exterior and interior landscape, maintenance, installation and design/build contractors.

Color Marketing Group
5904 Richmond Highway, Suite 408
Alexandria, VA 22303
T: 703.329.8500
F: 703.329.0155
www.colormarketing.org
Sets trends for popular colors.

Lighting Research Center
21 Union Street
Troy, NY 12180
T: 518.687.7100
F: 518.687.7120
www.lrc.rpi.edu
Research center advancing the effective use of light for society and the environment.

National Association of Homebuilders
1201 15th Street, NW
Washington, DC 20005
T: 800.368.5242
F: 202.266.8559
www.nahb.org
Promotes house building as a national priority; helps homeowners find qualified builders.

National Association of the Remodeling Industry
780 Lee Street, Suite 200
Des Plaines, IL 60016
T: 800.611.6274
F: 877.685.NARI
www.nari.org
Network of people who work in the remodeling industry.

National Guild of Professional Paperhangers
136 South Keowee Street
Dayton, OH 45402
T: 800.254.6477
or 937.222.6477
F: 937.222.5794
www.thepaperhangers.com
Access to nearly 1,000 paperhangers around the U.S.

National Kitchen & Bath Association
687 Willow Grove Street
Hackettstown, NJ 07840
T: 908.852.0033
F: 908.852.1695
www.nkba.org
Offers all the tips and tools for designing or renovating a kitchen or bath.

National Paint & Coatings Association (NPCA)
1500 Rhode Island Avenue, NW
Washington, DC 20005
T: 202.462.6272
F: 202.462.8549
www.paint.org
Advice on manufacturers and uses of their specific products.

Painting and Decorating Contractors of America (PDCA)
3913 Old Lee Highway, 2nd Floor
Fairfax, VA 22030
T: 703.383.0800
F: 703.359.2576
www.pdca.com
Offers a comprehensive nationwide database of professional, quality painters.

Tile Council of America
100 Clemson Research Blvd.
Anderson, SC 29625
T: 864.646.8453
F: 864.646.2821
www.tileusa.com
Comprehensive directory of American tile manufacturers and artistic tile makers.

Wallcoverings Association
401 North Michigan Avenue
Chicago, IL 60611
T: 312.644.6610
www.wallcoveringsassociation.org
Highly informative wallpaper guide, including terms, tips and helpful links.

CONTRACTORS

Art in Construction, Ltd.
Steven Balser
34 West 22nd Street, 6th Floor
New York, NY 10010
T: 212.352.3019
F: 212.989.4902
www.artinconstruction.com
Produces a wide range of surface textures in plasterwork.

Chezar Custom Construction, Inc.
Howard Chezar
248 East 32nd Street, Suite 2B
New York, NY 10016
T: 212.725.0467
F: 212.684.5316
hmchezar@mindspring.com
High-end residential construction, with a focus on New York City and the Berkshires of Massachusetts.

David Flaharty
1064 Magazine Road
Green Lane, PA 18054
T: 215.234.8242
Ornamental plasterer works with period interiors, executing elaborate ceiling medallions.

Lico Contracting, Inc.
29-10 20th Avenue
Astoria, NY 11105
T: 718.932.8300
F: 718.204.9817
General contracting and management company specializing in high-end residential renovations.

Thoughtforms Corporation Builders
Andrew Goldstein
543 Massachusetts Avenue
West Acton, MA 01720
T: 978.263.6019
F: 978.635.9503
www.thoughtforms-corp.com
General contracting firm specializing in the building of high-end custom homes and unique institutional buildings.

INTERIOR DESIGNERS

ACD New York
Anthony Cochran
121 West 27th Street,703
New York, NY 10001
T: 212.229.0110
F: 212.229.6805
www.acdnewyork.com
acd@acdnewyork.com
Great design, comfortable
living, and impeccable quality.

Barbara Barry
9526 Pico Boulevard
Los Angeles, CA 90035
T: 310.276.9977
F: 310.276.9876
info@barbarabarry.com
Number one LA-based designer,
renowned for creating glamorous
yet restful interiors.

Benjamin Huntington
Feng Shui & Design
271 Fifth Avenue
New York, NY 10016
T: 212.334.7762
F: 212.679.6011
fengshui-ny@juno.com
Professor, author, lecturer, interior
designer and founder of the
Mountain Institute of TriBeCa;
trained in both traditional and
contemporary Feng Shui.

Benjamin Noriega-Ortiz, LLC
Benjamin Noriega-Ortiz
75 Spring Street
New York, NY 10012
T: 212.343.9709
F: 212.343.9263
www.benjaminnoriegaortiz.com
Top designer with two master's
degrees in architecture, and an eye
for modern design, bold colors and
rich finishes.

Brooks & Orrick, Inc.
Monique Corbat-Brooks, AIA
Alicia Ritts Orrick
63 Pemberwick Road
Greenwich, CT 06831
T: 203.532.1188
F: 203.532.1180
Integrates architecture and
interior design, with a specialty in
personal attention.

Cullman & Kravis, Inc.
Elissa Cullman & Tracey Pruzan
790 Madison Avenue
New York, NY 10021
T: 212.249.3874
F: 212.249.3881
Exquisite traditional interior
design; specializes in working with
collections of fine art and antiques.

Drysdale Design Associates, Inc.
Mary Douglas Drysdale
Washington, DC
T: 202.588.0700
Leading designer with distinctive
and classically elegant interiors.

Easton Moss, Inc.
David Anthony Easton
72 Spring Street, 7th Floor
New York, NY 10012
T: 212.334.3820
F: 212.334.3821
Acknowledged master of eclectic
traditional interiors; recently part-
nered with Charlotte Moss, decora-
tor of classic English interiors.

Eve Robinson Associates
Eve Robinson
2112 Broadway, Suite 403
New York, NY 10023
T: 212.595.0661
F: 212.787.5021
everobinsonassoc@aol.com
Forward-thinking interior designer
who uses natural materials in
comfortable modern settings.

Glenn Gissler Design Inc.
Glenn Gissler
36 East 22nd Street,
8th Floor
New York, NY 10010
T: 212.228.9880
ggd36e22@aol.com
Primarily an interior designer, also
holds a degree in architecture; calm,
considered designs.

Jamie Gibbs & Associates
Jamie Gibbs
340 East 93rd Street
New York, NY 10128
T: 212.722.7508
F: 212.369.6332
Known for his classic, traditional
interiors.

Katie Ridder, Design & Decoration
Katie Ridder
1239 Broadway, Suite 1604
New York, NY 10001
T: 212.779.9080
www.katieridder.com
An expert at balancing the classical
with the unexpected to accomplish
a one-of-a-kind design.

Kitty Hawks, Inc.
Kitty Hawks
136 East 57th Street
New York, NY 10022
T: 212.832.3810
Classic interiors punctuated with
eclectic designs.

Miles Redd, Inc.
Miles Redd
300 Elizabeth Street
New York, NY 10012
T: 212.995.1922
mredd@nyc.rr.com
Designer with a devoted
following for his exuberant style
and elegant, updated interiors.

Matthew Patrick Smyth, Inc.
Matthew Patrick Smyth
12 West 57th Street
New York, NY 10019
T: 212.333.5353
F: 212.333.5093
www.matthewsmyth.com
Classic designer renowned for his
ability to incorporate clients'
specific interests into his designs.

Noel Jeffrey, Inc.
Noel Jeffrey
215 East 58th Street
New York, NY 10022
T: 212.935.7775
F: 212.935.8280
Noeljeff@aol.com
"Substantial comfort" is the
trademark of this seasoned
design expert.

Pierce Allen
DD Allen, Michael Pierce
80 8th Avenue, Suite 1602
New York, NY 10011
T: 212.627.5440
F: 212.727.1930
info@pierceallen.com
Interior designer and architect
team—leading edge style with
character and color.

Scott Salvator Interior Design
Scott Salvator
308 East 79th Street
New York, NY 10021
T: 212.861.5355
F: 212.861.9557
Formal, lavish, traditional interiors.

Solis Betancourt
Jose Solis Betancourt
1739 Connecticut Avenue, NW
Washington, DC 20009
T: 202.659.8734
F: 202.659.0035
jsolis@solisbetancourt.com
High-end residential interior
design.

Thomas Jayne Studio
Thomas Jayne
136 East 57th Street
New York, NY 10022
T: 212.838.9080
F: 212.838.9654
Renowned for historically accurate,
traditional interiors.

Victoria Hagan Interiors
Victoria Hagan
654 Madison Avenue, 2201
New York , NY 10021
T: 212.888.1178
www.victoriahagan.com
Elegant, eclectic, edited interior
design.

ZG Design
Zina Glazebrook
P.O. Box 144
Sagaponack, NY 11962
T: 631.537.4454
F: 631.537.4453
www.zgdesign.com
Full-service design firm with a flair
for primitive/modernist interiors
and an affinity for color.

CHAPTER TWO:
SITE & SCALE

LANDSCAPE ARCHITECTS & GARDEN DESIGNERS

Barbara Israel Garden Antiques
Barbara Israel
21 East 79th Street
New York, NY 10021
T: 212.744.6281
F: 212.744.2188
www.bi-gardenantiques.com
Specializes in fine antique garden
ornament from Europe and America.

Cole Creates
Rebecca Cole
41 King Street
New York, NY 10014
T: 212.255.4797
or 212.243.2849
info@colecreates.com
Garden and interior designer, as
well as author and co-host of TV's
Surprise by Design.

Finesse Landscape Design
Eric Hagenbruch
P.O. Box 711
St. James, NY 11780
T: 800.681.3463
or 631.862.9007
F: 631.862.4212
1finesse@optonline.net
Full-service landscape design firm,
specializing in natural landscapes.

John Jay Land Management
Jay Archer, Bill Meyer
282 Katonah Avenue, #268
Katonah, NY 10536
T: 914.232.0399
F: 845.278.0659
www.landdesign.net
Full-service landscape design firm.

Madison Cox Garden Design
220 West 19th Street
New York, NY 10011
T: 212.242.4631
F: 212.807.8081
Top-end designer who travels the
world to work on both private and
public gardens.

OUTDOOR/GARDEN FURNITURE

Brown Jordan International
9860 Gidley Street
El Monte, CA 91731
T: 800.743.4252
www.brownjordan.com
Collection of fine outdoor and
casual furniture.

Janus et Cie
8687 Melrose Avenue
West Hollywood, CA 90069
T: 310.652.7090
F: 310.652.1284
www.janusetcie.com
Renowned for high-quality garden
and casual furniture.

Mecox Gardens
257 County Road
Southampton, NY 11968
T: 631.287.5015
F: 631.287.5018
www.mecoxgardens.com
Unusual garden ornaments and
furniture as well as home furnishings. Online catalog available.

Munder-Skiles
799 Madison Avenue,
3rd Floor
New York, NY 10021
T: 212.717.0150
F: 212.717.0149
Creates period outdoor furniture
using the finest materials.

CHAPTER THREE: CRAFTING THE PLAN

APPLIANCES

ASKO USA, Inc.
P.O. Box 851805
Richardson, TX 75081
T: 800.898.1879
www.askousa.com
A complete line of high-performance washers, dryers and dishwash-
ers, built with Scandinavian quality
and environmental sensitivity.

Viking Range Corporation
111 Front Street
Greenwood, MS 38930
T: 888.VIKING
or 662.455.1200
www.vikingrange.com
Professional-grade appliances for
the home.

BATH & KITCHEN FIXTURES

American Standard
One Centennial Avenue
P.O. Box 6820
Piscataway, NJ 08855
T: 732.980.3000
F: 732.980.3335
www.americanstandard.com
The world's largest manufacturer
of bath and kitchen products.

Kohler Co.
444 Highland Drive
Kohler, WI 53044
T: 800.4KOHLER
www.kohlerco.com
A global leader in products for
the kitchen and bath.

CHAPTER FOUR: ARCHITECTURAL SOLUTIONS

ARCHITECTURAL SALVAGE

Irreplaceable Artifacts
216 East 125th Street
New York, NY 10035
T: 212.777.2900
F: 212.780.0642
www.irreplaceableartifacts.com
Offers architectural ornaments
from all over the world.

Urban Archaeology
143 Franklin Street
New York, NY 10013
T: 212.431.4646
F: 212.343.9312
www.urbanarchaeology.com
Committed to saving historic architectural elements; also has extensive reproduction line of lighting,
bathroom fittings and hardware.

METALWORK

Wainlands
453 West 17th Street
New York, NY 10011
T: 212.243.7717
F: 212.243.7722
www.wainlands.com
Can craft anything imaginable out
of metal.

HARDWARE SUPPLIERS

Baldwin Hardware Corporation
841 East Wyomissing Blvd.
P.O. Box 15048
Reading, PA 19612
T: 800.566.1986
F: 610.916.3230
www.baldwinhardware.com
An exceptional array of solid
brass products.

E.R. Butler & Co.
75 Spring Street, 5th Floor
New York, NY 10012
T: 212.925.3565
F: 212.925.3305
www.erbutler.com
Custom and high-end hardware.

P.E. Guerin, Inc.
23 Jane Street
New York, NY 10014
T: 212.243.5270
F: 212.727.2290
High-quality decorative hardware,
both classic and contemporary.

MOLDINGS

Dykes Lumber
1899 Park Avenue
Weehawken, NJ 07087
T: 201.867.0391
F: 201.867.1674
www.dykeslumber.com
Stocks over 300 moldings in both
wood and polymer; can purchase
online or by catalog.

**Hyde Park Fine Art of
Mouldings**
29-16 40th Avenue
Long Island City, NY 11101
T: 718.706.0504
F: 718.706.0507
www.hyde-park.com
Sculptural plaster moldings, both
in stock and custom.

TILE

Aliah Sage Studio
P.O. Box 758
Arroyo Seco, NM 87514
T: 505.776.1674
www.aliahsage.com
Well-known tile artist who does
indoor and outdoor murals, floors,
pools, kitchens and baths.

Ann Sacks
8120 NE 33rd Drive
Portland, OR 97211
T: 800.278.8453
F: 503.287.8807
www.annsacks.com
Hand-painted tiles in distinctive
patterns and colors, as well as
mosaics and antique limestone.

Waterworks
60 Backus Avenue
Danbury, CT 06810
T: 203.546.6000
F: 203.546.6001
www.waterworks.com
Extensive collection of tiles from
Europe and America, as well as a
line of bath fittings.

WINDOWS & DOORS

Panorama Windows Ltd.
767 East 132nd Street
Bronx, NY 10454
T: 718.292.9882
F: 718.402.5683
Favored resource for aluminum,
steel and wood windows, as well as
solid and veneered doors.

Pella
102 Main Street
Pella, Iowa 50219
T: 888.847.3552
www.pella.com
Premium-quality windows, entry
door systems, storm doors and
patio doors.

The Woodstone Company
Patch Road, P.O. Box 223
Westminster, VT 05158
T: 802.722.9217
F 802.722.9528
www.woodstone.com
High-performance, custom-pegged
mortise and tenon wooden
windows and doors, plus historic
restoration and replication.

WINE CELLARS

Design Build Consultants, Inc.
Evan Goldberg
100 Melrose Avenue, Suite 206
Greenwich, CT 06830
T: 203.861.0111
F: 203.861.0112
evang@evang.com
Custom wine cellars, from simple
closet spaces to lavish suites.

CHAPTER FIVE: THE MAGIC OF PAINT & WALLPAPER

PAINTERS

Chuck Hettinger
208 East 13th Street
New York, NY 10003
T: 212.614.9848
Top New York artisan, works with
many interior designers.

Fresco Decorative Painting Inc.
324 Lafayette Street
New York, NY 10012
T: 212.966.0676
F: 212.966.0756
Decorative studio with many
finishes to choose from.

**Grand Illusion
Decorative Painting, Inc.**
Pierre Finkelstein
20 West 20th Street,
Suite 1009
New York, NY 10011
T: 212.675.2286
F: 212.352.2058
Historic, French-trained decorative
painter; also author and instructor
in decorative finishes.

SilverLining Interiors
2112 Broadway, Suite 402
New York, NY 10023
T: 212.496.7800
F: 212.496.1012
Full-service shop, acting as both a
general and finish contractor.

Vesna Bricelj
260 West Broadway
New York, NY 10013
T: 212.966.7703
briceljv@aol.com
A decorative finishes artist who specializes in classical and whimsical
designs.

PAINT COMPANIES & DISTRIBUTORS

Benjamin Moore and Co.
51 Chestnut Ridge Road
Montvale, NJ 07645
T: 800.344.0400
F: 201.573.0046
www.benjaminmoore.com
Used extensively by designers.

Color Factory Collection
114 West Palisades Avenue
Englewood, NJ 07631
T: 201.568.2226
F: 201.568.0859
Supplier of Donald Kaufman's ready-made color paint.

Donald Kaufman Color
Donald Kaufman and Taffy Dahl
336 West 37th Street,
Suite 801
New York, NY 10018
T: 212.594.2608
or 800.977.9198
Color consultants who mix custom paint colors using fine art principles; also offer a range of 66 ready-made colors.

Eagle Paint & Wallpaper Co.
114 West Palisades Avenue
Englewood, NJ 07631
T: 201.568.6051
F: 201.568.0859
Manufactures Donald Kaufman Color Collection paints.

Farrow & Ball
Call for Distributors
T: 845.369.4912
F: 845.369.4913
www.farrow-ball.com
British traditional paint and wallpaper manufacturer.

Janovic/Plaza
3035 Thomson Avenue
Long Island City NY 11101
T: 800.772.4381
or 718.786.4444
www.janovic.com
www.janovicplaza.com
Ships top paints, including Benjamin Moore, Schreuder, Pittsburgh, Devoe and Ralph Lauren, anywhere in the U.S.

WALLPAPER

The Alpha Workshops
245 West 29th Street,
Suite 12A
New York, NY 10001
T: 212.594.7320
F: 212.594.4832
Hand-painted wallpapers and onsite faux painting.

Blonder Wallcoverings
3950 Prospect Avenue
Cleveland, OH 44115
T: 216.391.0363
F: 216.391.0660
www.blonderwall.com
85-year-old company with a wide range of product.

Bradbury & Bradbury
P.O. Box 155
Benicia, CA 94510
T: 707.746.1900
F: 707.745.9417
www.bradbury.com
Hand-printed, historic wallpapers.

Elizabeth Dow, Ltd.
155 Avenue of the Americas
New York, NY 10013
T: 212.219.8822
www.elizabethdow.com
Diverse selection of innovative, contemporary painted wallcovering designs. Trade only.

Gracie Studio
419 Lafayette Street
New York, NY 10003
T: 212.924.6816
www.graciestudio.com
Signature hand-painted wallpapers, many with an Asian motif; offers custom lacquer furniture and museum quality restoration.

Zuber & Cie
D&D Building
979 Third Avenue
New York, NY 10022
T: 212.486.9226
www.zuber.fr
Traditional wallpapers made by the same method for 200 years.

WALLPAPER HANGERS

Jim Yates
267 Watertank Hill Road
Johnson City, TN 37604
T: 423.929.8552
F: 423.929.0859
www.historicwallpapering.com
Specializes in working with historic and art wallpapers.

John Nalewaja
170 West 74th Street
New York, NY 10023
T: 212.496.6135
Specialist in new and old scenic wallpapers and canvases. Installs, removes and restores.

WRN Associates
65 South Prospect Street
P.O. Box 187
Lee, MA 01238
T/F: 413.243.3489
rmkelly@paper-hangings.com
Works with high-end designers and museums to restore and install historic wallpapers.

CHAPTER SIX: DECORATING DETAILS

ANTIQUES

www.1stdibs.com
Web site with over 400 European dealers of decorative arts; can search, negotiate and purchase all online.

Florian Papp
962 Madison Avenue
New York, NY 10021
T: 212.288.6770
F: 212.517.6965
www.florianpapp.com
Extensive inventory of classical English antiques.

H.M. Luther Antiques
61 East 11th Street
New York, NY 10003
T: 212.505.1485
F: 212.505.0401
18th and 19th century continental furniture.

Israel Sack
730 Fifth Avenue
New York, NY 10019
T: 212.399.6562
F: 212.399.9252
Top-level American antiques from the 17th to 19th century.

Lee Calicchio, Ltd.
134 East 70th Street
New York, NY 10021
T: 212.717.4417
F: 212.717.5755
Neoclassical French antiques, and art objects from the late 18th and 19th centuries.

Newel Art Galleries, Inc.
425 East 53rd Street
New York, NY 10022
T: 212.758.1970
F: 212.371.0166
www.newelantiques.com
Six floors of all types of antiques, from 17th century Renaissance to French 1940s.

William Lipton, Ltd.
27 East 61st Street
New York, NY 10021
T: 212.751.8131
F: 212.751.8133
17th-19th century Asian antiques, including Tansu chests, Buddha statues and Korean cabinets.

ANTIQUE RESTORATION

Carlton House Restoration
40-09 21st Street
Long Island City, NY 11101
T: 718.609.0762
Restores important and historic antiques of all kinds.

ARTISANS

Penn & Fletcher, Inc.
21-07 41st Avenue, 5th Floor
Long Island City, NY 11101
T: 212.239.6868
F: 212.239.6914
www.pennandfletcher.com
Fine embroidery for drapery borders, valances, furniture, bed linens and pillows.

Point.618, Inc.
344 West 38th Street
New York, NY 10018
T: 212.947.8143
F: 212.563.5370
Traditional gilding and decorative finishes for furniture; also creates decorative curtain hardware.

Yorkville Caning
31-04 60th Street
Woodside, NY 11377
T: 718.274.6464
F: 718.274.8525
www.yorkvillecaning.com
Finest quality French hand caning, rush work and wicker restoration.

BEDS

Charles H. Beckley, Inc.
979 Third Avenue
New York, NY 10022
T: 212.759.8450
F: 212.759.8806
Custom mattresses made to order. Trade only.

BEDDING

Frette
799 Madison Avenue
New York, NY 10021
T: 212.988.5221
F: 212.988.5257
www.frette.com
Superb quality couture bedding, made in Italy.

Muse Group, Ltd.
One Design Center Place
Boston, MA 02210
T: 617.330.7891
F: 617.330.7980
Contemporary-style bedding of the highest quality. Trade only.

Nancy Koltes at Home
31 Spring Street
New York, NY 10012
T: 212.219.2271
F: 212.219.2695
www.nancykoltes.com
Luxury linens and home products, made in Italy with an American sensibility.

Pratesi
829 Madison Avenue
New York, NY 10021
T: 212.288.2315
F: 212.628.4038
www.pratesi.com
Legendary linens.

CARPETS & RUGS

ABC Carpet & Home
881 Broadway
New York, NY 10003
T: 212.473.3000
www.abccarpetandhome.com
Emporium for fine floor coverings
since 1897. Also has a branch for
furniture and accessories.

Darius Decorative &
Antique Rugs
981 Third Avenue
New York, NY 10022
T: 212.644.6600
F: 212.644.6941
www.dariusrugs.com
Antique and decorative rugs in
unusual designs and sizes.

Doris Leslie Blau
724 Fifth Avenue
New York, NY 10019
T: 212.586.5511
F: 212.586.6632
www.dorisleslieblau.com
Antique carpets in soft palettes
with unusual design motifs.

Stark Carpet Corporation
979 Third Avenue
New York, NY 10022
T: 212.752.9000
High-end, custom-designed carpet.
Trade only.

CARPET RESTORATION

Restoration by Costikyan
28-13 14th Street
Long Island City, NY 11101
T: 800.247.RUGS
F: 718.726.1887
Ultimate resource for antique
carpet cleaning and restoration.

CURTAIN HARDWARE & OTHER
WINDOW SPECIALTIES

3M
Construction Markets Division
St. Paul, MN
T: 800.480.1704
www.3m.com
Call for local distributors of 3M
Scotch tint window film, which
protects against UV rays.

Joseph Biunno of
Finials Unlimited
129 West 29th Street
New York, NY 10001
T: 212.629.5630
F: 212.268.4577
Extensive array of finials, pulls,
rings and ormolu mounts with an
array of finishes.

Solar Window Tinting Services
1395-25 Lakeland Avenue
Bohemia, NY 11716
T: 631.218.8228
F: 631.218.8235
Installs UV film coatings on resi-
dential and commercial windows.

FABRICS

Bennison Fabrics, Inc.
76 Greene Street
New York, NY 10012
T: 212.941.1212
F: 212.941.5587
Informal florals and geometrics on
cotton and linen, made in England.

Bergamo Fabrics, Inc.
P.O. Box 231
Mt. Vernon, NY 10551
T: 914.665.0800
F: 914.665.7900
www.bergamofabrics.com
Contemporary and classic fabrics.
Trade only.

Brunschwig & Fils
979 Third Avenue
New York, NY 10022
T: 212.838.7878
F: 212.838.5611
www.brunschwig.com
High-end, traditional fabrics and
wallpapers. Trade only.

Chelsea Editions
232 East 59th Street
New York, NY 10022
T: 212.758.0005
F: 212.758.0006
Exquisite embroidered textiles and
crewelwork. Trade only, but can be
purchased retail through the store
in London, Chelsea Textiles,
T: (0)20 7584 0111.

DesignTex, Inc.
200 Varick Street, 8th Floor
New York, NY 10014
T: 212.886.8200
F: 212.797.4949
www.dtex.com
Contemporary and geometric
fabrics, including burnished
metallics. Trade only.

F. Schumacher & Co.
79 Madison Avenue
New York, NY 10016
T: 212.213.7900
www.fschumacher.com
Fine fabrics, mostly traditional.
Trade only.

Fortuny
979 Third Avenue
New York, NY 10022
T: 212.753.7153
F: 212.935.7487
www.fortuny.com
Large-scale, richly dyed cottons
mimicking the luster and look of
silk and velvet. Trade only.

Rose Brand
75 Ninth Avenue, 4th Floor
New York, NY 10011
T: 212.242.7554
or 800.223.1624
F: 212.242.7565
www.rosebrand.com
Theatrical equipment supplier
maintains stock of durable
fabrics, muslin, canvas and felt in
extra large widths.

Scalamandré
942 Third Avenue
New York, NY 10022
T: 212 980.3888
F: 212 688.7531
www.scalamandre.com
A complete source for high-end
designer fabrics, trimming and
wallpapers. Trade only, but offers
designer referral.

The Silk Trading Co.
Los Angeles, CA
T: 323.954.9280
or 800.371.0629
www.silktrading.com
Luxurious and affordable silks,
cottons and velvets available
either by retail or mail order.

FIREPLACE SURROUNDS
& MANTELS

Amazing Grates
61-63 High Road
London N2 8AB
United Kingdom
T: 020.8883.5556
www.amazing-grates.co.uk
Offers sleek, modern alternatives to
traditional mantels.

Barry H. Perry
19 East 65th Street, #4A
New York, NY 10021
T: 212.628.0489
F: 212.452.1625
Specialist in architectural antiques
such as period English and
French marble, stone and wood
chimney pieces.

Crea France US, Inc.
149 Reade Street
New York, NY 10013
T: 212.962.1211
F: 212.962.1997
www.creafrance.com
Specializes in reproduction antique
fireplaces.

William H. Jackson Company
21 East 58th Street
New York, NY 10022
T: 212.753.9400
F: 212.753.7872
Restores and sells antique mantels,
since 1827.

FURNITURE

George Smith
75 Spring Street
New York, NY 10012
T: 212.226.4747
F: 212.226.4868
www.georgesmith.com
Manufacturers and retailers of
handmade to order classic English
furniture and fabrics.

Holly Hunt
1728 Merchandise Mart
Chicago, IL 60654
T: 800.446.1313
F: 312.661.0243
www.hollyhunt.com
Contemporary furnishings and decorative accessories, including lighting and textiles.

Howard Kaplan Antiques
827 Broadway
New York, NY 10003
T: 212.674.1000
F: 212.228.7204
www.howardkaplanantiques.com
18th and 19th century, French,
English and decorative antiques, as
well as custom reproductions.

Niermann Weeks
232 East 59th Street
New York, NY 10022
T: 212.319.7979
F: 212.319.6116
www.niermannweeks.com
Designs, manufactures and distrib-
utes high-end, customized furniture, lighting, textiles and accessories. Trade only.

Saladino Group Inc.
200 Lexington Avenue
New York, NY 10016
T: 212.684.6805
Large-scale, high-backed furniture,
designed by famed interior designer
John Saladino.

Wood & Hogan
200 Lexington Avenue
New York, NY 10016
T: 212.532.7440
F: 212.532.4640
www.woodandhogan.com
Classic furnishings and accessories.
Trade only.

SPECIALTY ITEMS

ProSeal Plus, Inc.
1701 Westfork Drive, Suite 101
Lithia Springs, GA 30122
T: 800.754.0381
F: 770.941.8239
Seals fabrics and wallpapers
with a special finish; also laminates
fabrics.

TRIMMING

Houlès USA
8584 Melrose Avenue
Los Angeles, CA 90069
T: 310.652.6171
F: 310.652.8370
www.houles.com
A range of trimmings and fabrics
from France. Trade only, but will
advise on how to purchase.

M&J Décor
983 Third Avenue
New York, NY 10022
T: 212.704.8000
F: 212.704.8044
www.mjtrim.com
Enormous inventory of trimming.

UPHOLSTERERS

Flam Associates
Kenneth Flam
805 East 134th Street
Bronx, NY 10454
T: 718.665.3140
Upholsterer used by New York
interior designers, including
Benjamin Noriega-Ortiz.

La Chaise de France, Inc.
Dye Workers Building
1 Cottage Street
Easthampton, MA 01027
T: 413.529.1927
F: 413.529.1928
Specializes in traditional uphol-
stery treatment on historical
furniture. Trade only.

Soft Touch Designs
115 Labau Avenue
Staten Island, NY 10301
T: 718.448.1028
Specializes in custom slipcovers for
all types of upholstered items.

Versailles Drapery & Upholstery
37 East 18th Street, 9th Floor
New York, NY 10003
T: 212.533.2059
F: 212.995.1681
High-end upholstery in traditional
and modern fashion. Trade only.

CHAPTER SEVEN:
ART & ACCESSORIES

ART SERVICES

Albertson-Peterson Art
Consultants
P.O. Box 1900
Winter Park, FL 32790
T: 407.628.1258
F: 407.647.6928
www.albertsonpeterson.com
Escorts clients to museums and
galleries to educate on the purchas-
ing of art.

Art Advisory Services
Judith Selkowitz
530 Park Avenue
New York, NY 10021
T: 212.935.1272
F: 212.755.3924
www.artadvisoryservices.com
Expert and comprehensive advice
on artwork acquisition.

ILevel, Inc.
David Kassel
37 East 7th Street
New York, NY 10003
T: 212.477.4319
www.ilevel.biz
Leading art consultant—places
and installs all types of art.

I'll Hang For You
1804 Third Avenue
New York, NY 10029
T: 212.348.1225
Places and installs artworks.

Investment Interiors
Sylvia Leonard Wolf
160 West 77th Street
New York, NY 10024
T: 212.799.8009
F: 212.799.7675
Combines design services with
wise investment strategies for
building a valuable collection.

AUCTION HOUSES

Christie's
20 Rockefeller Plaza
New York, NY 10020
T: 212.636.2000
www.christies.com
Worldwide. Offers a wide range
of sales categories.

Sotheby's
1334 York Avenue
New York, NY 10021
T: 212.606.7000
www.sothebys.com
Worldwide. Offers a wide range
of sales categories.

FRAMING

J. Pocker & Son
135 East 63rd Street
New York, NY 10021
T: 212.838.5488
www.jpocker.com
Expert custom framing and matting.

CHAPTER EIGHT:
ILLUMINATION

LAMPSHADES

Oriental Lampshade Co.
816 Lexington Avenue
New York, NY 10021
T: 212.832.8190
F: 212.758.5367
www.orientallampshade.com
Offers a wide variety of ready-made
shades, as well as custom designs.

LIGHTING

Baldinger Architectural
Lighting, Inc.
19-02 Steinway Street
Astoria, NY 11105
T: 718.204.5700
F: 718.721.4986
www.baldinger.com
Finest decorative lighting made in
an artisan atmosphere.

Brass Light Gallery
P.O. Box 674
Milwaukee, WI 53201
T: 800.243.9595
F: 800.505.9404
www.brasslightgallery.com
Manufacturer of made-to-order
light fixtures; top quality, beautiful
designs.

The Lighting Center
240 East 59th Street
New York, NY 10022
T: 212.888.8388
F: 212.888.4689
General lighting resource,
offering everything to complete
a lighting plan.

Litelab Corp.
251 Elm Street
Buffalo, NY 14203
T: 800 238.4120
or 716.856.4491
F: 716.856.0156
www.litelab.com
Manufacturer of lighting for museum and retail applications, including the Litelab PictureWash™
Fixture.

Nulux Inc.
112 Green Street
Brooklyn, NY 11222
T: 718.383.1112
F: 718.383.1118
www.nulux.com
Architectural lighting fixtures
inspired by Edison Price.

Tailored Lighting, Inc. (SoLux®)
1350 Buffalo Road, Suite 12
Rochester, NY 14624
T: 800.254.4487
F: 585.328.2198
www.solux.net
Manufacturer of lighting, including
MR-16 halogen lamps and the
SoLux® Art Light.

LIGHTING DESIGNERS

Hillmann DiBernardo &
Associates, Inc.
Carl Hillmann, LC, IALD, IES
134 West 26th Street
New York, NY 10001
T: 212.529.7800
F: 212.979.9108
carl@hdalight.com
Works with top architects on
all types of projects, including
residential.

Johnson Schwinghammer
Lighting Design Consultants, Inc.
Bill Schwinghammer
335 West 38th Street, Suite 1
New York, NY 10018
T: 212.643.1552
F: 212.643.1553
www.jslighting.com
High-quality lighting design firm
with a reputation as one of the
country's leaders.

Landscape Illumination
Greg Yale
27 Henry Road
Southampton, NY 11968
T: 631.287.2132
F: 631.287.2182
Travels nationwide, using the
latest technology to create
effective lighting solutions
outdoors.

Lighting Collaborative
Lewis Herman
124 West 24th Street, Suite 6C
New York, NY 10011
T: 212.627.5330
F: 212.645.2815
lightingcollab@mindspring.com
Lighting design firm for high-end
residential clients, specializing in
lighting artwork.

INDEX

PHOTOGRAPHY CREDITS